10-MINUTE NUMBER GAMES for Clever Kids

Puzzles and solutions
by Dr Gareth Moore
B.Sc (Hons) M.Phil Ph.D

Illustrations and cover
artwork by Chris Dickason

Designed by Tall Tree Ltd

10-MINUTE NUMBER GAMES for Clever Kids

Buster Books

First published in Great Britain in 2022 by Buster Books,
an imprint of Michael O'Mara Books Limited,
9 Lion Yard, Tremadoc Road, London SW4 7NQ

W www.mombooks.com/buster

F Buster Books

Y @BusterBooks

O @buster_books

Clever Kids is a trade mark of Michael O'Mara Books Limited.

Puzzles and solutions © Gareth Moore

Illustrations and layouts © Buster Books 2022

A CIP catalogue record for this book is available from the British Library.

ISBN: 978-1-78055-888-2

1 3 5 7 9 10 8 6 4 2

This product is made of material from well-managed FSC®-certified
forests and other controlled sources. The manufacturing processes conform
to the environmental regulations of the country of origin.

Printed and bound in October 2022 by
CPI Group (UK) Ltd, Croydon, CRO 4YY.

FSC
www.fsc.org

MIX
Paper from
responsible sources
FSC® C171272

INTRODUCTION

Get ready to push your brain to the limit and test your number skills with these fun-filled games!

Take your pick of over 100 number puzzles. You can complete them in any order you like and work through the book at your own pace.

Start each puzzle by reading the instructions. Sometimes this is the hardest part of the puzzle, so don't worry if you have to read the instructions a few times to be clear on what they mean.

Once you're clear on what to do, it's time to battle your way to the answer. Can you complete each puzzle in ten minutes or less? Time yourself and write down how long each game took you in the space provided.

For an extra challenge, you can come back to the puzzles at a later date and see if you can complete them even faster.

If you really struggle with a puzzle, take a look at the solutions at the back to see how it works, then try it again later and see if you can work it out the second time round.

Good luck, and have fun!

**Introducing the Number Games Master:
Gareth Moore, B.Sc (Hons) M.Phil Ph.D**

Dr Gareth Moore is a number games genius, and author of lots of puzzle books.

He created an online brain-training site called BrainedUp.com, and runs a puzzle site called PuzzleMix.com. Gareth has a Ph.D from the University of Cambridge, where he taught machines to understand spoken English.

Can you find all of the listed numbers in the grid? They can be written in any direction, including diagonally, and can be read either forwards or backwards.

15698	375072	692230	898520
200953	493379	732199	949678
262787	524119	818289	9632
328191	529960	894654	990581

2	6	2	7	8	7	0	7	4	9
4	2	2	6	8	6	9	9	2	8
2	5	7	0	9	7	3	3	9	2
3	8	6	9	0	3	6	8	5	8
2	1	2	4	7	9	5	9	2	1
8	5	7	9	9	2	5	2	4	8
1	6	0	3	0	8	5	3	1	9
9	9	5	9	9	0	5	8	1	3
1	8	7	7	3	2	1	9	9	2
8	5	3	9	6	9	2	2	3	0

Can you work out which of these animals is the fastest, using the clues below?

Clues:

The animal's number:

- Is not a multiple of 5

- Is not a number with two identical digits, such as 11 or 22

- Is not a multiple of 3

- Is not a number that ends in a '4'

The animal's number is: ....

NUMBER GAME 3

How quickly can you fill in these number pyramids? Each block should contain a number equal to the sum of the two blocks immediately beneath it.

Here's an example to show what a complete pyramid looks like:

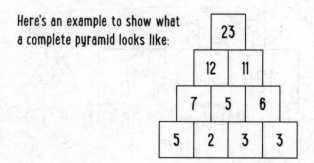

a)

NUMBER GAME 4

Can you solve these Sudoku puzzles? Just place a number from 1 to 6 into every empty square, so that no number repeats in any row, column or bold-lined 3x2 box.

Here's an example solved puzzle, so you can see how it works:

6	3	2	4	1	5
1	4	5	3	6	2
5	6	3	2	4	1
2	1	4	5	3	6
3	2	1	6	5	4
4	5	6	1	2	3

Row → · Column ↑ · Box ↑

a)

6		2	3		4
4		3	6		5
2	6			4	3
3	4			5	6
1		4	5		2
5		6	4		1

b)

		6	4		
	4			1	
2		4	6		1
3		1	5		4
	2			4	
		5	2		

c)

					1
		3			6
				6	4
2	6				
5			3		
3					

See if you can solve these brain chains in your head, without writing down any numbers until the final answer. Start with the value at the top of each puzzle, then follow each arrow in turn and do what the mathematical instruction says until you reach the 'Result' box. Write the final value you end up with in that box.

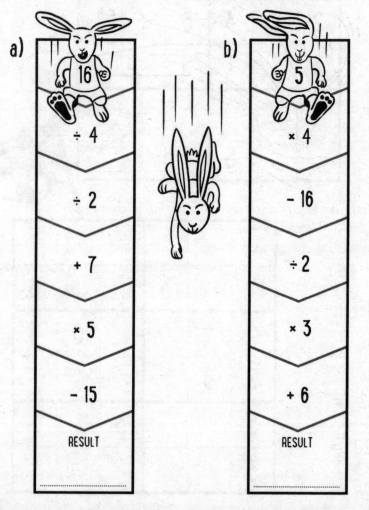

a)

16

÷ 4

÷ 2

+ 7

× 5

− 15

RESULT

....

b)

5

× 4

− 16

÷ 2

× 3

+ 6

RESULT

....

Each of the following balloons has a different number on it.

You want to buy a selection of balloons which adds up to each of the totals below. For each purchase, you can buy no more than one of each value of balloon. Which balloons should you pick? The first one is done for you as an example.

Totals:

10 = 4 + 6

12 = _____ + _____

20 = _____ + _____ + _____

26 = _____ + _____ + _____ + _____

If you start at the square marked 'X', and follow the sequence of movements shown, at which of the lettered squares do you end up? Each arrow represents moving one square in the direction shown. There are a lot of arrows, so you will need to be careful not to lose track of the path!

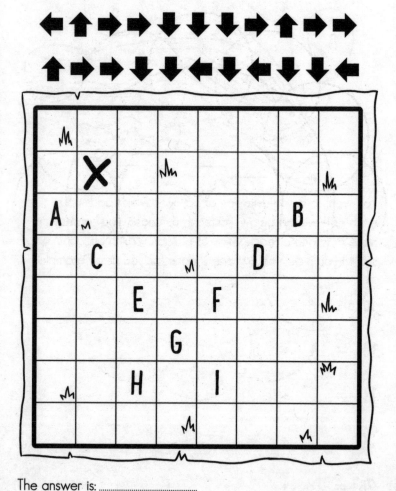

The answer is: ....

What is the smallest possible number of circles that could have been used to create this picture?

The answer is: _____

To solve the puzzles on this page, you'll need to know that there are 31 days in December and January. But you probably knew this already.

a) If it's the 1st of April today, how many days is it until the 25th of April?

....

b) If yesterday was the 2nd of January, how many days is it until the 3rd of February?

....

c) In five days it will be the 1st of January. How many days ago was the 25th of December?

....

Each book on these shelves has a different number on it.
They have been arranged in a particular order on each shelf.

Can you write in the number that is missing from the blank
book on each shelf? Each shelf uses its own mathematical rule.

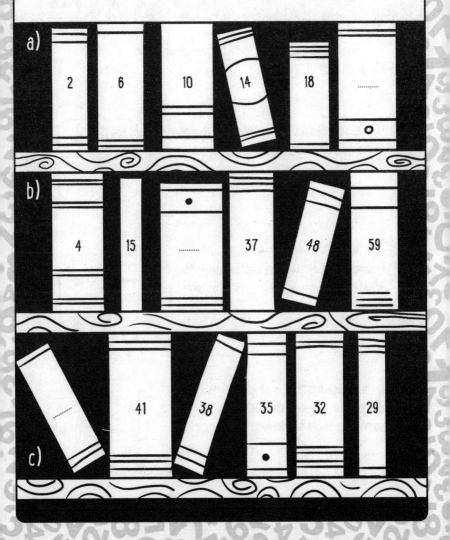

a) 2   6   10   14   18   .... (o)

b) 4   15   .... (•)   37   48   59

c)   41   38   35 (•)   32   29

You have several six-sided dice whose faces once looked like this, representing 1 to 6 in turn:

Unfortunately, some of the dots have been rubbed off some of the dice.

a) If you saw the following face, which looks like a 3, how many other numbers could it be? What are they?

....

b) On another dice you see the following face. What possible numbers could it represent?

....

c) A third dice has just a single dot in the centre. What is the highest number it could represent?

....

Imagine that each of the speedy objects below represents a different number. Can you use the sums to work out the value of each object, and write these values at the bottom of the page?

🛼 + 🚀 = 12

🚀 + 🛼 + 🛼 = 19

🛼 + 🚀 + 🚀 = 17

🛼 = ...   🚀 = ...

Draw lines along some of the grid lines to divide the grid up into a set of rectangles and squares, so that every grid square is inside exactly one shape. Each shape must also contain exactly one number, and that number must be equal to the number of grid squares inside that shape.

Take a look at this example to see how the puzzle works:

The calculation below is wrong because 3 x 5 does not equal 18. Can you change one of the numbers in the calculation into a different number by adding just **one** straight line, so that the calculation is then correct?

$$3 \times 5 = 18$$

Now add **two** straight lines to fix this second calculation:

$$2 \times 6 = 15$$

Place a number from 1 to 4 into each empty square, so that no number repeats in any row, column or bold-lined 2x2 box. These numbers must be placed, however, so that the two numbers nearest to the end of each row or column add up to the number just outside the grid.

Take a look at this example to see how the puzzle works:

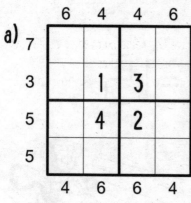

Notice how these numbers add up to 3

... and these add up to 6

a)

b)

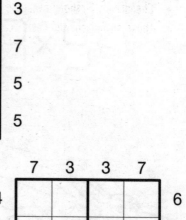

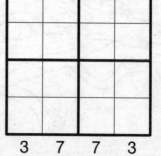

Adrian, Beau and Chandrika are celebrating their birthdays today. Can you work out how old each animal is from the following information?

- Each age is a single-digit number (that is, a number from 1 to 9)

- The number of candles that will go on each animal's birthday cake will match their age

- Chandrika is three times as old as Beau is

- In six years' time, Beau will be the same age that Chandrika is now

- Chandrika's birthday cake will have the same number of candles as those on Adrian' and Beau's cakes added together

Adrian is: ....

Beau is: ....

Chandrika is: ....

Solve these Futoshiki puzzles by placing a number from 1 to 5 into each empty square, so that no number repeats in any row or column. You must also follow the 'greater than' signs - these are arrows which tell you which is the larger number in some pairs of squares. The arrow always points to the smaller number.

Take a look at this example to see how it works:

a)

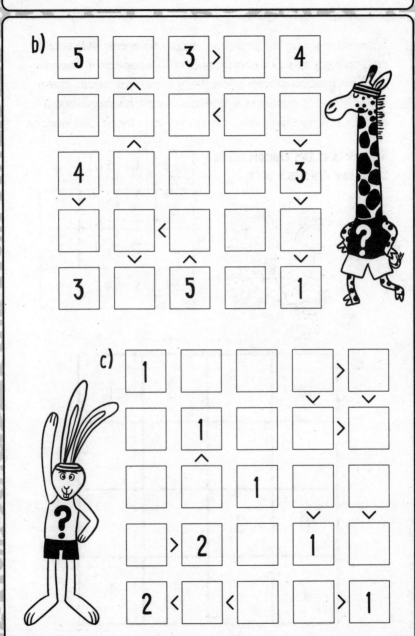

Can you write a number in each empty square so that each grid contains every number from 1 to 16 once each? The numbers must be placed so that they form a path from 1 all the way to 16, moving only between touching squares but without moving diagonally.

Take a look at this example solution to see how the puzzle works:

15	14	9	8
16	13	10	7
1	12	11	6
2	3	4	5

a)

16		12	1
8	9		
7			4

b)

16	1		
15			
	11		5
13		7	

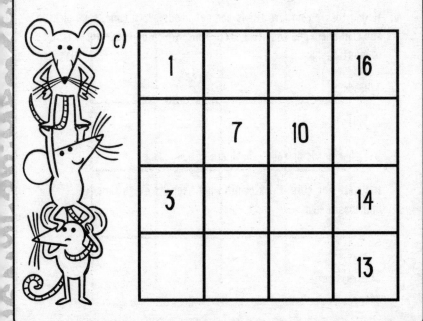

c)

1			16
	7	10	
3			14
			13

If you toss a coin one time, it has an equal chance of landing either heads up or tails up. But what about if you toss it more than once?

a) If you toss a coin twice in a row, what is the chance that you get the same result both times? That is, two tails or two heads? If you're not sure, try writing down the possible results of each toss and counting how many possible outcomes there are.

The answer is: ....

b) If you toss a coin five times and get heads every time, then pick up the coin again and toss it a sixth time, which of these three results is most likely:

1. Heads

2. Tails

3. Either heads or tails – both are equally likely

If you're not sure, think about what happens every time you toss a coin.

The answer is: ....

Have a go at fitting all the listed numbers into the grid, writing one digit per square so that every number can be read either across or down the grid. Cross off each number as you place it. One is placed already to get you started.

| | | 5 | 2 | 4 | 0 | 0 |

3 Digits	5 Digits	6 Digits	7 Digits
836	18564	154098	1393501
870	19184	621044	4864455
	40946		
	~~52400~~		

Imagine placing these two pictures on top of each other, so the white squares on one image are filled with the contents of the corresponding non-white squares in the other. Then answer the questions below.

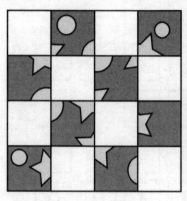 

a) How many circles are there?

....

b) How many stars are there?

....

Can you form each of the given totals, by choosing one number from each ring of this dartboard?

For example, you could form a total of 9 by picking 1 from the innermost ring, 5 from the middle ring and 3 from the outermost ring.

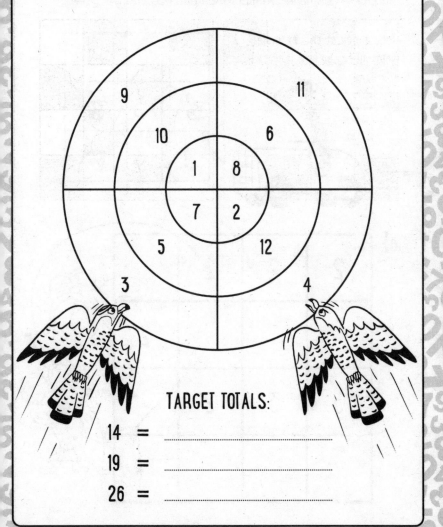

TARGET TOTALS:

14 = ...

19 = ...

26 = ...

Can you use the number clues to work out which grid squares contain hidden flags? Each number tells you exactly how many flags there are in its touching squares, including diagonally touching squares. Flags can only be placed in the empty squares, and there can never be more than one flag in any square.

Take a look at this example solution to see how it works:

		1
🏁	3	🏁
1	3	🏁

a)

2	2	2	
			2
3	3	2	

b)

2	2		
			2
3	4		2
		2	

c)

2	2		
		2	
	4	2	
1			1

See if you can place all of the given dominoes into each grid, using each domino exactly once. Draw along the dashed lines to mark the borders of the dominoes, and cross them out once you've used them. One is already placed in each puzzle to get you started.

Here's an example solution:

1	2	3	4		
3	3	2	3	3	
4	1	4	2		
1	4		4	1	3
1	4	2	1	2	2

a)

	2	3	1	4	2
3		3			1
1	1	4	3	3	3
1	4	4	4		1
2		2	2	4	2

b)

1	2	1	4	3	
1	1	4	4		3
2	3	4	2	3	3
3				2	2
2	4		1		4	1

Which of the following numbers is the odd one out, and why?

The answer is: ....

Try the following calculations, all to do with time, and see how you get on.

a) If you have breakfast at 8:00am and then have lunch 5 hours later, at what time do you have lunch?

....

b) If you also had a mid-morning snack exactly halfway between breakfast and lunch, at what time did you have that?

....

c) If breakfast took 10 minutes to eat, lunch took twice as long, and the mid-morning snack took only half as long as breakfast to eat, then how long in total have you spent eating?

....

Place the numbers 1, 2 and 3 once each into every row and column within the grid. This means that one square will remain empty in each row and column. The closest digit to the start or end of a row or column must match the digit given outside the grid.

The bottom row of clues have been labelled with arrows in the example solution to the right, to show how they apply to the grid.

	2	3	1	1	
2	2	3	1		1
3	3		2	1	1
1		1	3	2	2
1	1	2		3	3

① ② ③ ③

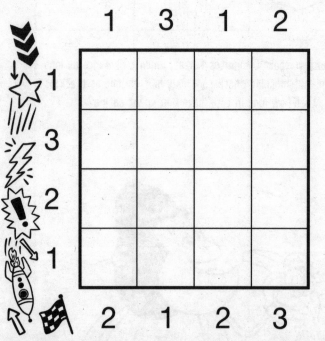

Can you solve these brain chains in your head, without writing down any numbers until the final answer? Start with the value at the top of each chain, then follow each arrow in turn and do what the mathematical instruction says until you reach the 'Result' box. Write the final value you end up with in that box.

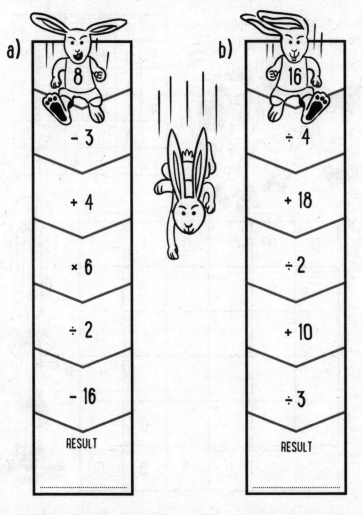

a)

8

− 3

+ 4

× 6

÷ 2

− 16

RESULT

....

b)

16

÷ 4

+ 18

÷ 2

+ 10

÷ 3

RESULT

....

Place either 0 or 1 into each empty square so that there are an equal number of '0's and '1's in each row and column. You must do this in such a way that there are never more than two '0's or two '1's next to each other within any single row or column.

Here's an example solution, so you can see how it works:

0	0	1	1	0	1
0	0	1	0	1	1
1	1	0	1	0	0
0	1	0	0	1	1
1	0	1	1	0	0
1	1	0	0	1	0

a)

0	0			0	1
	0			0	1
1					0
0					1
1	1			0	
	1	0		0	0

b)

1	0				1
		1		1	0
		0		1	
	0		1		
1	1		1		
0				1	0

c)

	0			1	1
		1	0		1
1	1		1		
		0		1	0
1		1	0		
1	1			0	

Can you draw a train track that travels through some of the squares, so that the track enters in the left column where shown and then exits in the bottom row as also shown? Some track pieces are given already.

The numbers at the start of each row and column tell you how many track pieces there must be in that row or column. Tracks can only go straight through a square or turn a corner – so they cannot cross over.

Take a look at this example to see how a completed puzzle works:

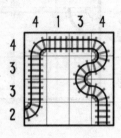

a)

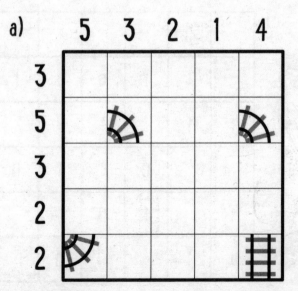

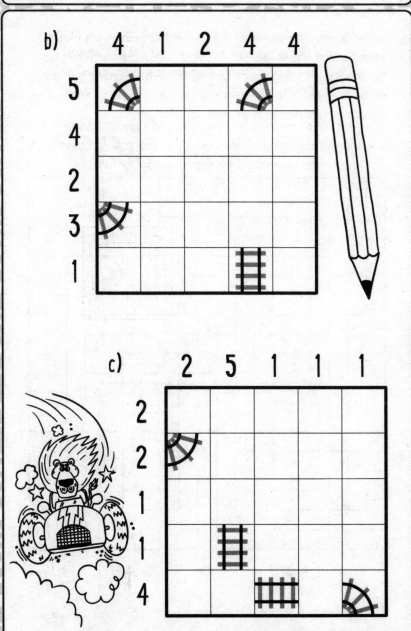

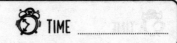

There is only one direct route through this maze, from the entry arrow at the top to the exit arrow at the bottom, which does not involve retracing your steps at all. Without drawing in the maze, can you find that direct route - and then say what all of the numbers it passes over add up to?

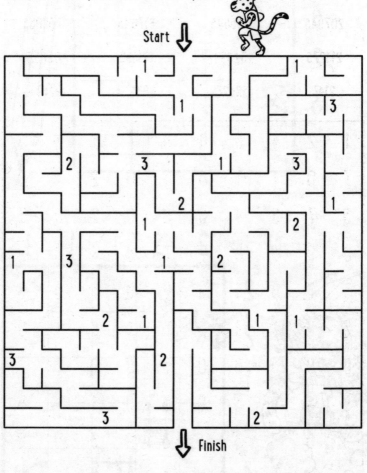

The answer is: ....

Can you find all of the listed numbers in the grid? They can be written in any direction, including diagonally, and can be read either forwards or backwards.

157085	326975	598403	698501
207945	335593	617845	739055
213275	34654	671698	888517
2147	528213	689334	973950

1	2	4	5	4	8	7	1	6	3
7	0	1	1	8	1	0	2	1	0
5	7	5	4	5	8	0	2	0	3
6	9	3	8	7	7	8	7	0	2
5	7	8	3	9	2	0	5	6	6
5	3	1	4	5	6	1	8	1	9
0	9	5	6	0	5	9	0	5	7
9	5	3	5	9	3	9	1	7	5
3	0	8	4	3	8	9	3	9	9
7	7	1	4	2	1	3	2	7	5

See how quickly you can solve these Sudoku puzzles. Just place a number from 1 to 6 into every empty square, so that no number repeats in any row, column or bold-lined 3x2 box.

Here's an example solved puzzle, so you can see how it works:

6	3	2	4	1	5
1	4	5	3	6	2
5	6	3	2	4	1
2	1	4	5	3	6
3	2	1	6	5	4
4	5	6	1	2	3

Row ⟶ (points to row 5 6 3 2 4 1)

Column ⟶ (points to first column, value 4)

Box ⟶ (points to bottom-right box)

a)

	1			2	
3					1
		5	4		
		2	3		
6					4
	4			5	

b)

		1	4		
	4			2	
1		5	6		2
4		2	3		5
	5			6	
		6	2		

c)

			5		
3		6			
	3				2
6				1	
			2		4
		4			

Can you draw lines to connect each pair of identical numbers together? The lines must not cross or touch each other, and only one line is allowed in each grid square. You can't use diagonal lines.

This example solution shows how it works:

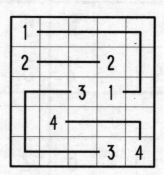

a)

b)

				1	2
1					
3		3			
			4	5	
	2				
			5	4	

c)

					1
2					
3		4	5		
				4	2
	3	5	1		

Can you place a number from 1 to 3 into each square so that no number repeats in any row or column?

These numbers must be placed so that each bold-lined area fulfils the mathematical result given at the top-left of that area:

- If the area has a '+' sign, the numbers in the region must add to the total shown.

- If the area has a '−' sign, one number in the region must subtract from the other to give the result shown.

- If the area has a '×' sign, the numbers in the region must multiply to the total shown.

- If the area has a '÷' sign, one number in the region must divide the other to give the result shown.

To see how this works, look at this example solution:

5+ 3	2	12× 1
1	3	2
2	2− 1	3

Notice how the digits in the '5+' area add up to 5, and how the digits in the '12×' area multiply to make 12. Notice also how in the '2-' area you can subtract 1 from 3 to give a result of 2.

a)

3÷		9+
	6×	

b)

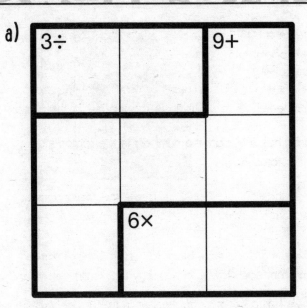

18×		6×
2×		

The picture to the right shows a 3x3x3 tower of blocks, containing 27 blocks in total.

You build three more identical block towers, then take some blocks away from each tower. How many blocks are left in each pile now?

a)

.... blocks left

b)

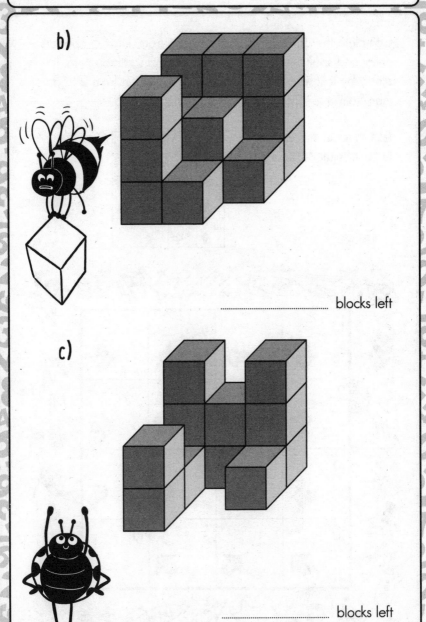

.... blocks left

c)

.... blocks left

Complete the grid so that each number from 1 to 16 appears once, and so that you can trace a path from 1 through to 16 simply by following the arrows from 1 to 2, then from 2 to 3, then from 3 to 4, and so on all the way up to 16.

Take a look at this example to see how the puzzle works:

1 ↘	12 ➡	7 ↙	13 ↙
11 ↗	2 ↓	14 ↙	6 ↙
8 ↘	3 ↙	5 ↗	15 ↓
10 ↑	9 ←	4 ↑	16

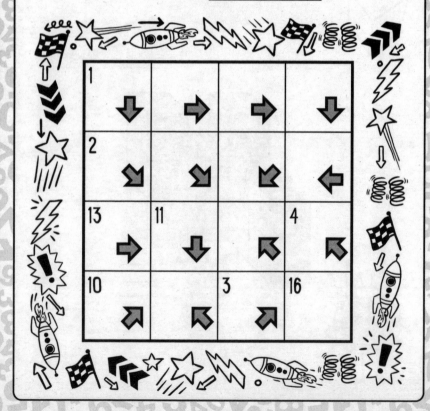

1 ↓	➡	➡	↓
2 ↘	↘	↙	←
13 ➡	11 ↓	↖	4 ↖
10 ↗	↖	3 ↗	16

Imagine placing these two pictures on top of each other, so the white squares on one image are filled with the contents of the corresponding non-white squares in the other.

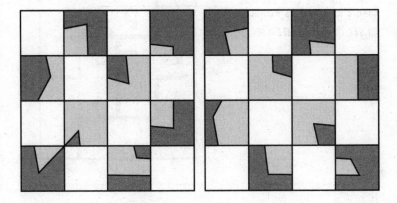

In this imaginary combined image, how many sides does the light-shaded shape have?

....

Can you draw along some of the dashed lines to divide each grid into four separate areas? Every area must contain the numbers 1 to 4 once each.

Take a look at this example solution to see how the puzzle works:

4	3	4	1
2	3	3	2
4	1	4	2
2	3	1	1

a)

2	4	1	2
3	3	1	3
1	1	4	3
4	4	2	2

b)

1	4	1	2
2	3	2	3
1	1	3	4
4	3	4	2

c)

1	2	4	4
3	4	3	1
4	2	3	3
2	1	1	2

Can you draw lines to connect each pair of identical numbers together? The lines must not cross or touch each other, and only one line is allowed in each grid square. You can't use diagonal lines.

This example solution shows how it works:

1						1
2		2				
			3	1		
		4				
				3	4	

a)

		1	2			
1			3		4	
			5			
	5		3			6
6	4				2	

b)

	1					
				2		
1	3					
				4		
5						3
2		4				5

c)

		1				
	2			3		
	4					
						3
		5				
						4
1	2		5			

Can you write a number in every empty square, so that in each pyramid all of the blocks that have two blocks beneath them contain a number equal to the sum of the numbers in those two blocks?

Here's an example to show what a complete pyramid looks like:

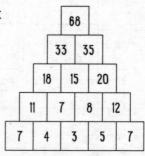

a)

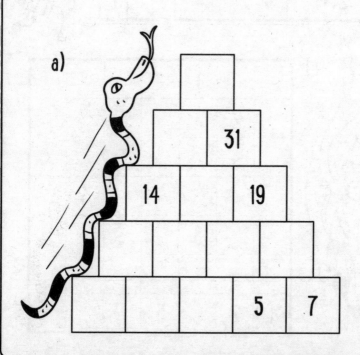

See if you can place a number from 1 to 4 into each square, so that no number repeats in any row, column, bold-lined 2x2 box or dashed-line cage.

The numbers in each dashed-line cage must add up to the total given at the top-left of that cage.

Take a look at this example solved puzzle to see how it works:

a)

Place the numbers 1, 2 and 3 once each into every row and column within the grid. This means that one square will remain empty in each row and column. The closest digit to the start or end of a row or column must match the digit given outside the grid.

The bottom row of clues have been labelled with arrows in the example solution to the right, to show you how they apply to the grid.

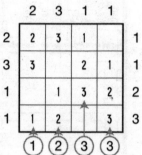

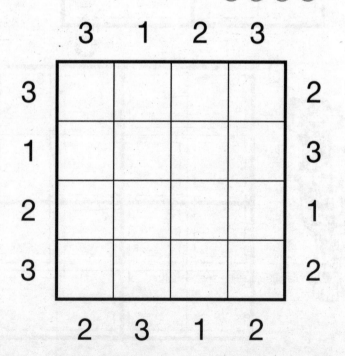

Using the clues below, can you work out which of these animals is going to win the race?

Clues:

The winning car has a number that:

- Is not a multiple of 7

- Is not a multiple of 9

- Is not an even number

- Is not a number where the first digit is higher than the second digit, such as 21 or 73

The answer is: ....

Can you solve these Sudoku puzzles? Just place a number from 1 to 9 into every empty square, so that no number repeats in any row, column or bold-lined 3x3 box.

a)

9			1	8	5			7
	5	8	2		9	3	6	
	1	4		6		9	5	
6	4		5		2		9	3
8		3		9		5		4
5	9		4		8		7	6
	6	5		2		7	3	
	8	9	7		6	4	1	
4			9	1	3			5

b)

1		8		9		4		6
	9		8		7		3	
3			4		1			9
	1	5				3	9	
9								8
	6	2				1	5	
7			6		2			3
	3		1		9		4	
5		1		4		9		2

What is the smallest possible number of five-pointed stars that could have been used to create this picture?

The answer is: ....

If you start at the square marked 'X', and follow the sequence of movements shown, at which of the lettered squares do you end up? Each arrow represents moving one square in the direction shown. There are a lot of arrows, so you will need to be careful not to lose track of the path!

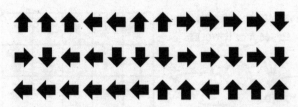

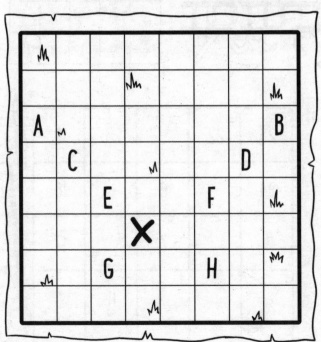

The answer is: ....

Write a number in each empty square so that each grid contains every number from 1 to 25 once each. The numbers must be placed so that they form a path from 1 all the way to 25, moving only between touching squares but without moving diagonally.

Take a look at this example solution to see how it works:

1	2	19	20	25
4	3	18	21	24
5	6	17	22	23
8	7	16	15	14
9	10	11	12	13

a)

25	22			19
24		8		18
1		7		17
			11	
		13		

b)

5		7		23
	1		25	
				21
	11		19	
13		15		

c)

5		3	2	1
				10
19		17		11
	21			
25				13

Each of the following balloons has a different number on it.

You want to buy a selection of balloons which adds up to each of the totals below. For each purchase, you can buy no more than one of each value of balloon. Which balloons should you pick? The first one is done for you as an example.

Totals:

21 = 4 + 17

25 = ... + ...

36 = ... + ... + ...

47 = ... + ... + ... + ...

Which of the following numbers is the odd one out, and why?

As a clue, the solution to this puzzle involves thinking about the individual digits that make up each of the numbers.

The answer is: ....

For instructions please see Number Game 35. In this version, however, you must now place 1 to 4 once each in every row and column. The other rules remain the same.

a)

6×		5+	
4×	6+		6×
	4+		
12×		2÷	

b)

72×			4×
	1−	8×	
3−			18×

c)

6×		2÷	
6×			4×
	12+		
5+			

d)

24×			4÷
8×		18×	
4÷			
	6×		

Can you form each of the given totals by choosing one number from each ring of this dartboard?

For example, you could form a total of 9 by picking 3 from the innermost ring, 4 from the middle ring and 2 from the outermost ring.

TARGET TOTALS:

12 = ...

25 = ...

30 = ...

The calculation below is wrong, because 4 + 0 does not equal 12. Change one of the numbers in the calculation into a different number by adding just **one** straight line, so that the calculation is then correct.

$$4 + 0 = 12$$

Now add **two** straight lines to one of these three numbers to fix this second calculation:

$$5 - 5 = 3$$

Fit all of the listed numbers into the grid, writing one number per square so that every number can be read either across or down the grid. Cross off each number as you place it.

4 Digits	5 Digits	7 Digits
4664	68807	4028696
8150		6687209
9386		8166463
9902		

Different countries often have different 'time zones', depending on where they are in the world. For example, when it's 2pm in Britain it will be 3pm in France, or it might be 2am in New Zealand. The exact differences between countries can vary, depending on the seasons.

a) If it's 9am in Britain, and French time is one hour ahead of British time, then what time is it in France?

....

b) When it's midnight in New York City, on the east coast of the United States, it's 9pm in Los Angeles, on the west coast. So, if it's now midday in Los Angeles, what time is it in New York City?

....

c) At 4pm in Britain, it's 6pm in Egypt but only 1pm in Brazil. So, if it's now 7pm in Cairo, Egypt, then what time is it in Rio de Janeiro, Brazil?

....

Can you use the clues to work out which grid squares contain hidden flags? Each number tells you exactly how many flags there are in its touching squares, including diagonally touching flags. Flags can only be placed in the empty squares, and there can never be more than one flag in any square.

Take a look at this example solution to see how it works:

		1
🏁	3	🏁
1	3	🏁

a)

2	3		1
			1
3		2	
	2		

b)

		2	
1			2
	1		
1		2	1

c)

2				1
3		4		3
		2		
	4			
	3		2	1

Place either 0 or 1 into each empty square so that there are an equal number of '0's and '1's in each row and column. You must do this in such a way that there are never more than two '0's or two '1's next to each other within any single row or column.

Here's an example solution, so you can see how it works:

0	0	1	1	0	1
0	0	1	0	1	1
1	1	0	1	0	0
0	1	0	0	1	1
1	0	1	1	0	0
1	1	0	0	1	0

a)

		1		1	1
1	1				
0		0	1	0	
	0	1	1		1
				1	0
1	0		1		

b)

	0			0	1
0		0			1
	0	1		0	0
0	1		0	1	
1			1		1
1	1			1	

c)

	0	0		0	0	1	1
	0		0	1	1		
		1		0			0
				1			1
0			0				
0			1		1		
		0	1	0		1	
1	1	0	0			1	0

Place a number from 1 to 9 in each white square, so that each 'run' of continuous horizontal or vertical white squares adds up to the number given to the left or the top of that run. No number can repeat within a run, so a clue of '4' must be solved with 1 and 3, and never with 2 and 2.

Notice how the 1 and 2 add up to 3

Notice how the 2, 1 and 3 add up to 6

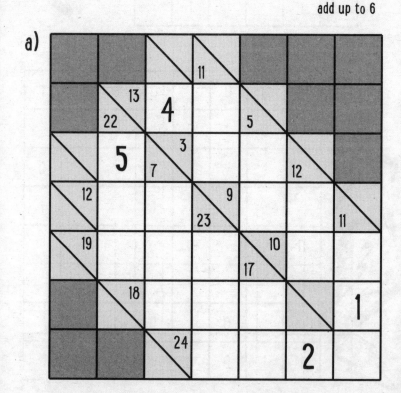

a)

b)

		13		11	4	6
	20		**9**			
10	**1**		7			
	6	10			12	
		6				
3	6					
7			10			**1**
15				**5**		

Can you solve these brain chains in your head, without writing down any numbers until the final answer? Start with the value at the top of each chain, then follow each arrow in turn and do what the mathematical instruction says until you reach the 'Result' box. Write the final value you end up with in that box.

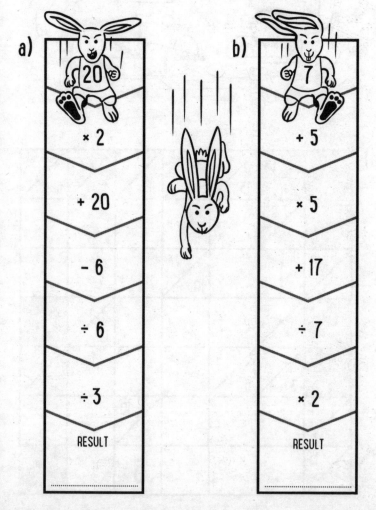

a)

20

× 2

+ 20

− 6

÷ 6

÷ 3

RESULT

....

b)

7

+ 5

× 5

+ 17

÷ 7

× 2

RESULT

....

Imagine that each of the speedy objects below represents a different number. Can you use the sums to work out the value of each object and write these in the gaps at the bottom of the page?

🛼 + ⚙ = 11

🛼 + 🚀 = 7

🚀 + ⚙ = 12

🛼 + 🚀 + ⚙ = 15

 = ...   = ...   = ...

Place all of the given dominoes into each grid, using each domino exactly once. Draw along the dashed lines to mark the borders of the dominoes, and cross them out once you've used them. One is already placed in each puzzle, to get you started.

Here's an example solution:

1	2	3	4		
3	3	2	3	3	
4	1	4	2		
1	4		4	1	3
1	4	2	1	2	2

a)

	1		1		2
4	4		1	4	2
2	2		4	2	3
	3	1	4	1	3
1	4	3	3	3	2

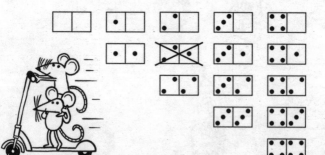

b)

1	1	1	5	6	2	6	1
5	5	4	**2**		2	4	1
3	5	3	**5**	5	4	3	2
3	6	1	5	4	4	6	4
1	3	3	1	2			2
	3	5	6	6	4	6	2
	3	2	4			6	

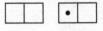

Solve these Futoshiki puzzles by placing a number from 1 to 5 into each empty square, so that no number repeats in any row or column. You must also follow the 'greater than' signs - these are arrows which tell you which is the larger number in some pairs of squares. The arrow always points to the smaller number.

Take a look at this example to see how it works:

2	3	4	5	1
1 < 4	5	2 < 3

a)

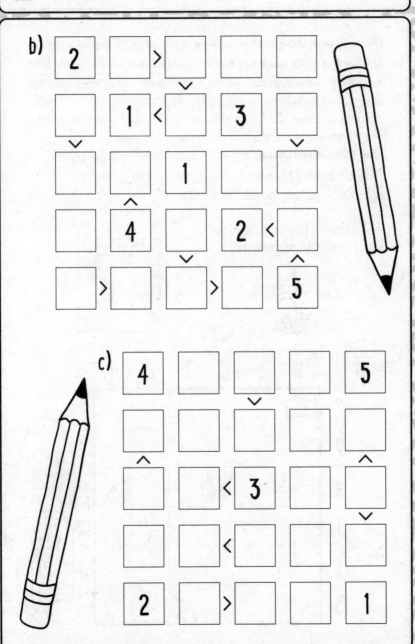

Draw a train track that travels through some of the squares, so that the track enters in the left column where shown and then exits in the bottom row as also shown. Some track pieces are given already.

The numbers at the start of each row and column tell you how many track pieces there must be in that row or column. Tracks can only go straight through a square or turn a corner – so they cannot cross over.

Take a look at this example to see how a completed puzzle works:

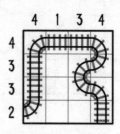

a)

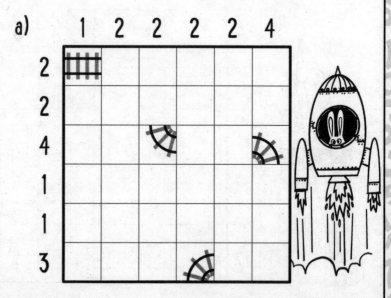

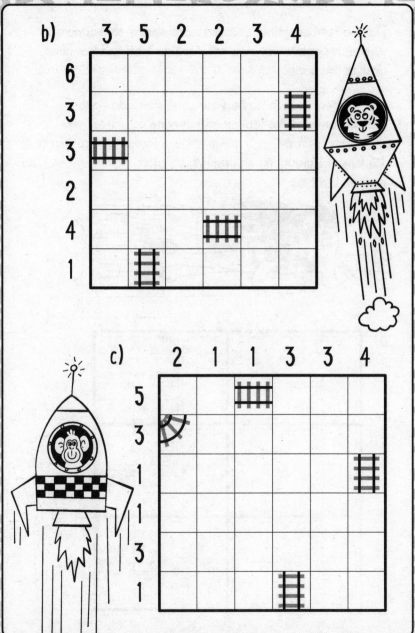

Place a number from 1 to 6 into each square, so that no number repeats in any row, column, bold-lined 3x2 box or dashed-line cage.

The numbers in each dashed-line cage must add up to the total given at the top-left of that cage.

See Number Game 42 for a solved example using numbers 1 to 4.

a)

14	3		10	10	
	7				6
	7		6		
6	9		4		12
	12	5	7		
			8		

b)

⌐8	⌐5	⌐9		⌐5	
			⌐15		
⌐3		⌐9	⌐5	⌐10	
⌐9				⌐6	
⌐12			⌐12	⌐6	⌐4
⌐8					

c)

⌐16		⌐8		⌐11	⌐8
			⌐8		
⌐11				⌐7	
⌐15		⌐13			
	⌐6		⌐20		
		⌐3			

Draw along some of the dashed lines to divide the grid into a set of squares and/or rectangles, so that each of these shapes contains exactly one number. That number must be equal to the width plus the height of the shape, measured in grid squares.

Take a look at the example to the right to see how it works.

This rectangle is 3 squares wide and 5 tall, which add up to 8

a)

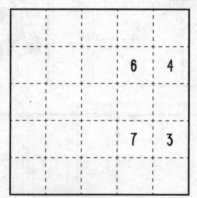

b)

If you fold a square of paper in half, then in half again, you end up with a smaller square. Now fully unfold it and you end up with a square with two crease lines in it, like this:

Here's another piece of paper that has been folded up and then unfolded, leaving the crease lines shown. Can you work out how many times it was folded, before it was unfolded? Assume it wasn't folded more than necessary to make the pattern shown.

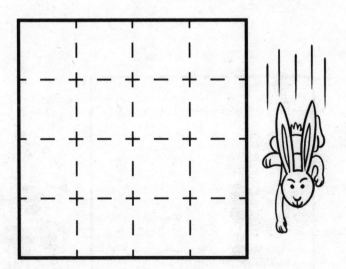

The answer is: ....

Draw along some of the dashed lines to divide each grid into four separate areas. Every area must contain the numbers 1 to 4 once each.

Take a look at this example solution to see how the puzzle works:

4	3	4	1
2	3	3	2
4	1	4	2
2	3	1	1

a)

4	4	1	2
3	2	1	3
4	1	3	2
4	3	1	2

b)

4	3	4	2
4	2	1	1
2	4	1	3
3	1	2	3

In this third puzzle, you must divide the grid into six separate areas:

c)

1	4	2	4	2	3
2	3	3	4	2	1
2	3	2	1	1	3
1	4	3	1	4	4

Can you draw lines to connect each pair of identical numbers together? The lines must not cross or touch each other, and only one line is allowed in each grid square. You can't use diagonal lines.

This example solution shows how it works:

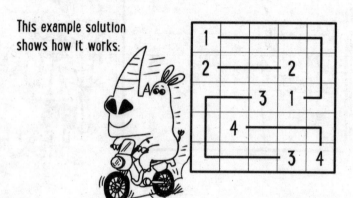

a)

		1					1	
		2	3			4		
				5				
				6				
				7				
						7		3
	4			2		5		6

b)

	1			2	3		
			4			4	
		3					
1		5			6	7	6
				7			
2		8				8	9
5		9					

c)

1		2					
3						4	
	5		4	5	6		
		1				2	6
				7			
	7	8					
						8	
	3						

Can you find all of the listed numbers in the grid? They can be written in any direction, including diagonally, and can be read either forwards or backwards.

105223	26300	5329	668642
105548	420958	570430	819347
195118	442911	582997	937997
197644	502128	662327	975514

2	7	2	5	2	6	6	2	3	2	7	3
4	6	4	9	9	3	7	9	9	7	0	0
1	3	1	2	2	7	9	4	5	2	2	3
2	1	9	9	0	3	5	6	1	2	8	0
8	2	1	7	7	9	5	1	0	5	1	9
7	1	0	9	5	6	5	4	5	8	9	5
5	4	1	0	6	5	4	8	5	2	3	5
7	5	0	5	3	2	1	4	4	9	4	0
0	1	0	4	9	6	9	4	8	9	7	2
4	4	1	1	1	1	2	8	7	7	1	1
3	9	1	2	4	6	8	6	6	2	5	2
0	0	2	3	2	2	2	5	0	1	4	2	8

You have several six-sided dice whose faces once looked like this, representing 1 to 6 in turn:

Unfortunately, some of the dots have been rubbed off some of the dice.

a) If you saw the following two faces:

- What is the highest total they could represent? ....

- And what is the lowest total they could represent? ....

b) On two further dice you see the following faces:

- What is the highest total they could represent? ....

- And what is the lowest possible total? ....

Place all of the given dominoes into each grid, using each domino exactly once. Draw along the dashed lines to mark the borders of the dominoes, and cross them out once you've used them. One is already placed in each puzzle to get you started.

Here's an example solution:

1	2	3	4		
3	3	2	3	3	
4	1	4	2		
1	4		4	1	3
1	4	2	1	2	2

a)

	1			4	2
1	4		2	2	
3	4	3	4		2
3	1	3	1	3	2
4	2	3	1	1	4

b)

4	3	2	5	1	3	1	
1	6	5	6	5	4	1	6
		5	2	5	3	1	6
6	5		6	6	1	4	3
	2	3	3	4		3	4
6		1	3	1	2	2	4
4	2	4		5	5	2	2

Can you solve these Sudoku puzzles? Just place a number from 1 to 9 into every empty square, so that no number repeats in any row, column or bold-lined 3x3 box.

a)

6								7
		7	1	3	6	8		
	1		7		2		5	
	6	8	2	1	7	5	4	
	9		4		5		7	
	4	5	8	9	3	2	6	
	2		6		9		8	
		4	5	2	1	7		
1								5

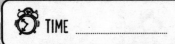
b)

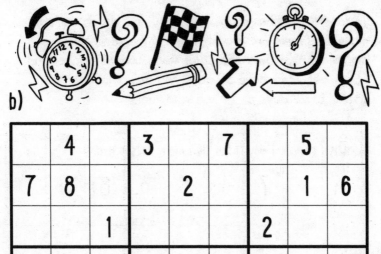

	4		3		7		5	
7	8			2			1	6
		1				2		
5			1		9			3
	3						9	
9			4		2			8
		5				6		
6	9			5			8	2
	2		6		8		7	

To solve the puzzles on this page, you'll need to know how many days there are in each month of the year. All of the months have 31 days, except for April, June, September and November, which have 30 days; and except for February which has 28 days, or 29 in a leap year.

a) If it's the 5th of May today, how many days is it until the 7th of July?

....

b) If in five days it will be the 3rd of April, then how many days is it until the 5th of April next year? Assume that next year is *not* a leap year.

....

c) Tomorrow is the 17th September. How many days ago was the 1st of June?

....

Each book on these shelves has a different number on it. They have been arranged in a particular order on each shelf.

Can you write in the number that is missing from the blank book on each shelf? Each shelf uses its own mathematical rule.

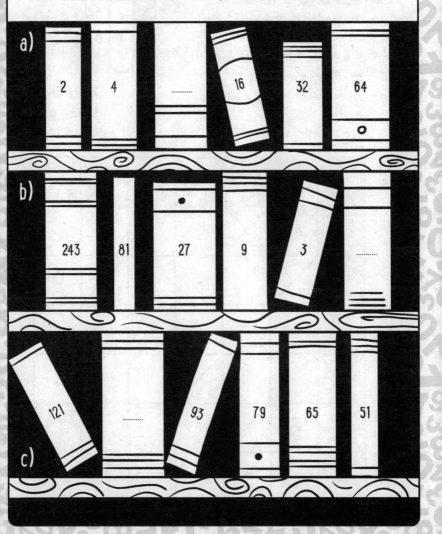

a) 2   4   16   32   64

b) 243   81   27   9   3   ....

c) 121   93   79   65   51

Place a number from 1 to 9 in each white square, so that each 'run' of continuous horizontal or vertical white squares adds up to the number given to the left or the top of that run. No number can repeat within a run, so a clue of '4' must be solved with 1 and 3, and never with 2 and 2.

Notice how the 1 and 2 add up to 3

Notice how the 2, 1 and 3 add up to 6

a)

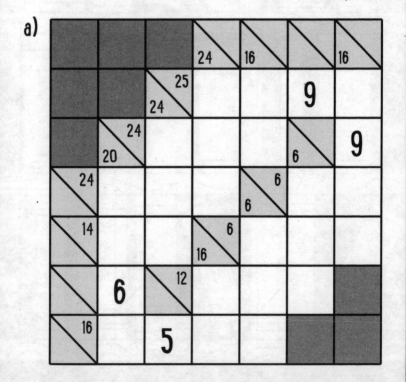

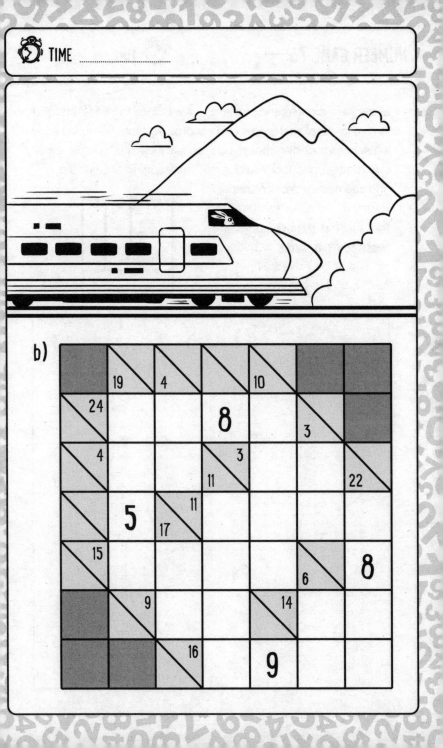

TIME ....

b)

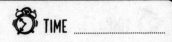
Draw lines along some of the grid lines so as to divide the grid up into a set of rectangles and squares, so that every grid square is inside exactly one shape. Each shape must also contain exactly one number, and that number must be equal to the number of grid squares inside that shape.

Take a look at this example to see how this works:

			6	3			3
				6			
8							
		5					5
	2		3				
			4		4		
					12		
3							

Place a number from 1 to 6 into each empty square, so that no number repeats in any row, column or bold-lined 3x2 box. These numbers must be placed, however, so that the three numbers nearest to the end of each horizontal row, and the two numbers nearest to the end of each vertical column, add up to the number just outside the grid.

Take a look at Number Game 15 for an example using a 4x4 grid.

a)

	3	11	7	7	7	7	
10			4	2			11
11							10
7	4					5	14
14	6					2	7
11							10
10			1	6			11
	8	6	7	7	7	7	

b)

	9	9	3	7	9	5	
13			2	1			8
8							13
7	1					5	14
14	5					4	7
8							13
13			6	5			8
	6	4	11	9	5	7	

Write a number in every empty square, so that in each pyramid all of the blocks that have two blocks beneath them contain a number equal to the sum of the numbers in those two blocks.

Here's an example to show what a complete pyramid looks like:

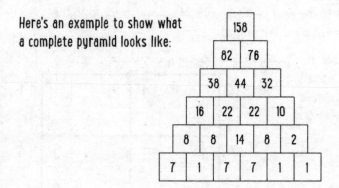

a)

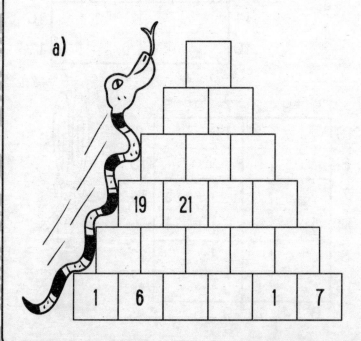

Write a number in each empty square so that each grid contains every number from 1 to 25 once each. The numbers must be placed so that they form a path from 1 all the way to 25, moving only between touching squares but without moving diagonally.

Take a look at this example solution to see how the puzzle works:

1	2	19	20	25
4	3	18	21	24
5	6	17	22	23
8	7	16	15	14
9	10	11	12	13

a)

	13			22
1			24	
	11			
		5		

Solve these Futoshiki puzzles by placing a number from 1 to 6 into each empty square, so that no number repeats in any row or column. You must also follow the 'greater than' signs – these are arrows which tell you which is the larger number in some pairs of squares. The arrow always points to the smaller number.

Take a look at this example to see how it works:

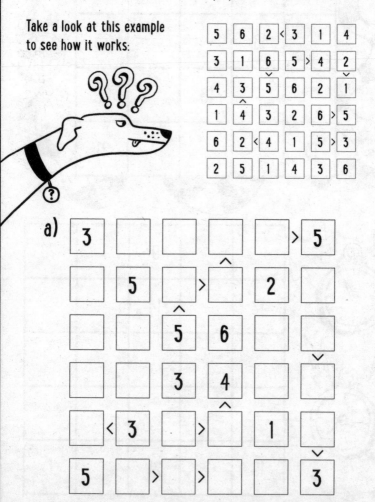

b)

	3			< 2	
3		2	5		4
	< 5			3	
	< 4		∧	∧ 6	
2		3	4 <		6
	2			4	

c)

5			>		> 3
			>		
∧		<		>		∧
				> ∨	
∨		>	∧			∧
2			∧		< 4

Diego, Eva and Freya are all celebrating their birthdays today. Can you work out how old each chimp is from the following information?

- All of the chimps are in the age range of 5 to 16.

- If Freya was half as old as she is today, she would be celebrating the same age as Eva.

- In two years' time, Diego will be the same age that Freya is today.

- If you add the ages of all three chimps together, the total is 28.

Diego is: ....

Eva is: ....

Freya is: ....

There is only one direct route through this maze, from the entry arrow at the top to the exit arrow at the bottom, which does not involve retracing your steps at all. Without drawing in the maze, can you find that direct route - and then say what all of the numbers it passes over add up to?

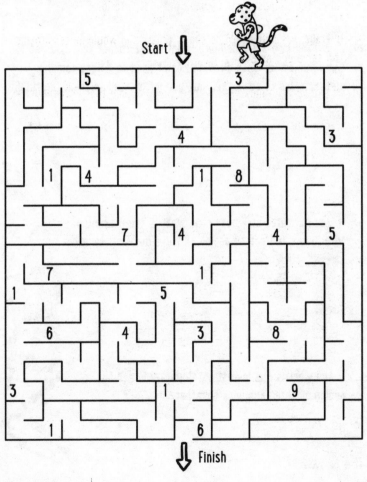

The answer is: ....

If you roll a normal six-sided dice, it has an equal chance of resulting in a 1, 2, 3, 4, 5 or 6. You can't roll any other number. This means you have a 1 in 6 chance of rolling any given one of those numbers. For example, you have a 1 in 6 chance of rolling a 4.

a) If you roll two six-sided dice, what is the chance that you get the same number on both dice? You don't need to do any complex mathematics to solve this, but you might need to think carefully.

The answer is: ....

b) If you roll three six-sided dice, what is the maximum total you could get by adding all three numbers together?

The answer is: ....

... And what is the lowest total you could get by adding all three numbers together?

The answer is: ....

Place a number from 1 to 4 into each empty square, so that no number repeats in any row, column or bold-lined 2x2 box. Also, the number placed in each circle must be equal to the sum of all of the numbers along the length of its attached arrow.

In this example solution, notice how the 1, 1 and 2 on the arrow add up to the circled 4.

For instructions please see Number Game 35. In this version, however, you must now place 1 to 5 once each in every row and column. The other rules remain the same.

a)

20×		9+	4×	
12×				60×
	30×			
	7+	16×		
			5×	

b)

11+	4÷		12+	
				2−
2−	2−			
	80×	18×		
		2÷		

c)

4−	5+	4÷	2−	
			16+	8×
6×				
		15×	10×	3×
4×				

d)

11+		24×		6×
6×		40×		
			4×	
6+	12×		13+	

 TIME ....

Can you form each of the given totals by choosing one number from each ring of this dartboard?

For example, you could form a total of 14 by picking 7 from the innermost ring, 2 from the middle ring and 5 from the outermost ring.

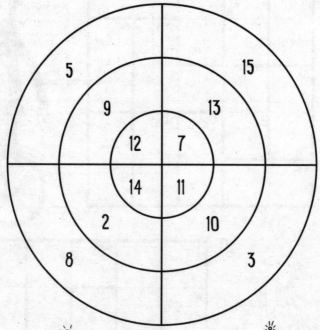

TARGET TOTALS:

20 = ...

33 = ...

38 = ...

Draw along some of the dashed lines to divide the grid into a set of squares and/or rectangles, so that each of these shapes contains exactly one number. That number must be equal to the width plus the height of the shape, measured in grid squares.

Take a look at the example to the right to see how it works.

This rectangle is 3 squares wide and 5 tall. which add up to 8

Place the numbers 1, 2 and 3 once each into every row and column within the grid. This means that two squares will remain empty in each row and column. The closest digit to the start or end of a row or column must match the digit given outside the grid.

Take a look at the example solution to the right to see how the puzzle works.

	2	2	2	1	3	
2			2	1	3	3
2	2		3		1	1
3	3	2	1			1
1		1		3	2	2
1	1	3		2		2
	1	3	1	2	2	

	3	3	2	3	1	
3						1
2						1
1						3
1						3
3						2
	1	1	3	1	2	

Each of the following balloons has a different number on it.

You want to buy a selection of balloons which adds up to each of the totals below. For each purchase, you can buy no more than one of each value of balloon. Which balloons should you pick? The first one is done for you as an example.

Totals:

10 = 3 + 7

17 = ... + ...

25 = ... + ... + ... + ...

32 = ... + ... + ... + ...

Can you use the clues to work out which grid squares contain hidden flags? Each number tells you exactly how many flags there are in its touching squares, including diagonally touching squares. Flags can only be placed in the empty squares, and there can never be more than one flag in any square.

Take a look at this example solution to see how it works:

a)

2			1
2		3	
2			1
	2		1

b)

			2	2
3	3	3		
			5	4
2				
	2	2	4	

c)

	2	2		1
1				1
	3		3	
				2
2	2		2	

The picture to the right shows a 4x4x3 tower of blocks, containing 48 blocks in total.

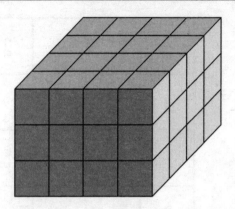

You build three more identical block towers, then take some blocks away from each tower. How many blocks are left in each pile now?

a)

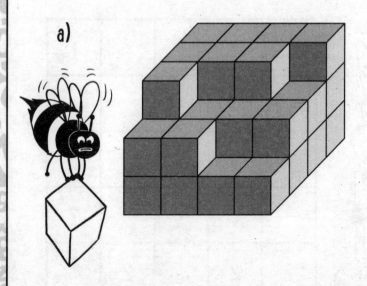

.... blocks left

b)

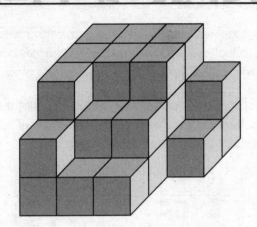

 .... blocks left

c)

.... blocks left

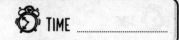
Fit all of the listed numbers into the grid, writing one digit per square so that every number can be read either across or down the grid. Cross off each number as you place it.

Getting started can be a bit tricky, so begin by placing the 7-digit numbers. There's only one way to place them which will let you fit in the numbers that need to cross over them.

3 Digits		4 Digits	5 Digits	7 Digits
167	582	1448	82529	7118982
202	629	1904	88444	7499593
209	697	5839		
212	795	7569		
372	859			
472	941			
504	942			

If you fold a square of paper in half, then in half again, you end up with a smaller square. Now fully unfold it and you end up with a square with two crease lines in it, like this:

Here's another piece of paper that has been folded up and then unfolded, leaving the crease lines shown. Can you work out how many times it was folded, before it was unfolded? Assume it wasn't folded more than necessary to make the pattern shown.

The answer is: ....

Place a number from 1 to 9 in each white square, so that each 'run' of continuous horizontal or vertical white squares adds up to the number given to the left or the top of that run. No number can repeat within a run, so a clue of '4' must be solved with 1 and 3, and never with 2 and 2.

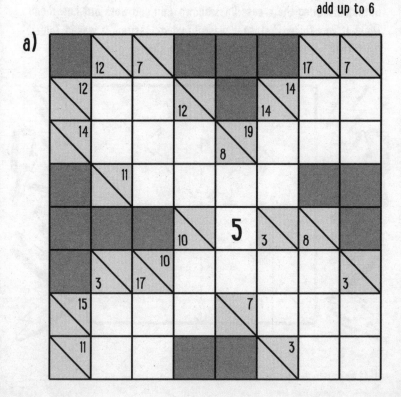

a)

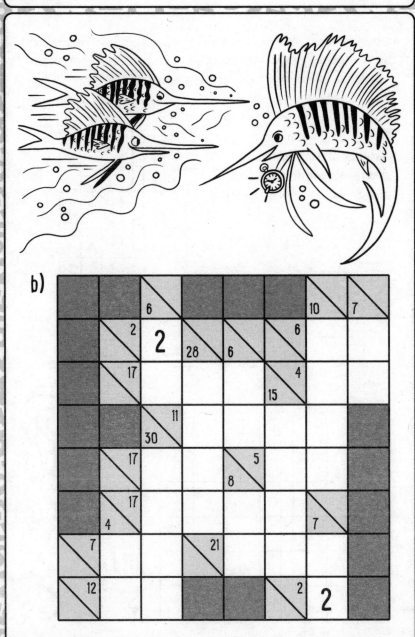

b)

Place either 0 or 1 into each empty square so that there are an equal number of '0's and '1's in each row and column. You must do this in such a way that there are never more than two '0's or two '1's next to each other within any single row or column.

Here's an example solution, so you can see how it works:

0	0	1	1	0	1
0	0	1	0	1	1
1	1	0	1	0	0
0	1	0	0	1	1
1	0	1	1	0	0
1	1	0	0	1	0

a)

		0	1	0	
		1			
	0	1		1	1
1	0		1	0	
			0		
	1	0	1		

b)

	1				0	0	
		0		1			1
0	0					1	
		0	1	0	1	0	0
1	0	1	0	1	0		
	0					1	0
0			0		0		
	0	1				0	

c)

1		0	1		0	1	1
							1
0		0		0		1	0
			0				1
0				0			
1	0		0		0		1
0							
1	1	0		0	1		0

The calculation below is wrong because 1 + 5 does not equal 1.

Can you add **two** straight lines, to change one or two of the numbers, so that the calculation is then correct?

$$1 + 5 = 1$$

And can you again add **two** straight lines, to change one or two of the numbers, so that the following calculation is correct too?

$$5 \times 9 = 48$$

Place a number from 1 to 6 into each empty square, so that no number repeats in any row, column or bold-lined 3x2 box. Also, the number placed in each circle must be equal to the sum of all of the numbers along the length of its attached arrow.

In this example solution, notice how the 1 and 2 on the top-left arrow add up to the circled 3.

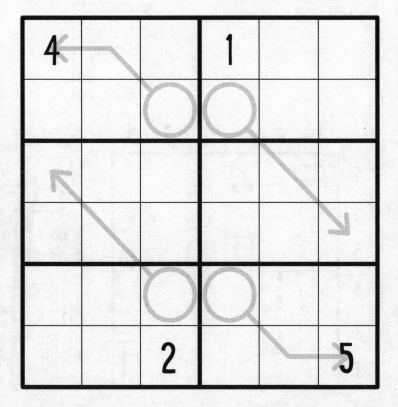

Draw a train track that travels through some of the squares, so that the track enters in the left column where shown and then exits in the bottom row as also shown. Some track pieces are given already, in the first two puzzles.

The numbers at the start of each row and column tell you how many track pieces there must be in that row or column. Tracks can only go straight through a square or turn a corner – so they cannot cross over.

Take a look at this example to see how a completed puzzle works:

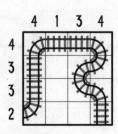

a)

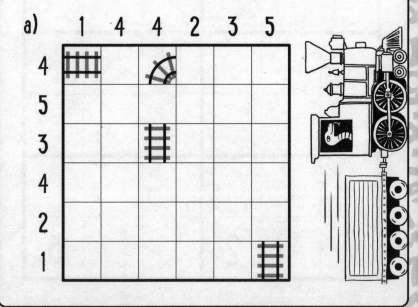

b)

	2	1	2	2	4	2
1	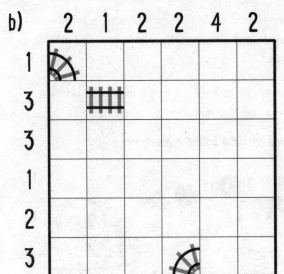					
3						
3						
1						
2						
3						

c)

	6	3	1	1	1	6
6						
2						
3						
3						
2						
2						

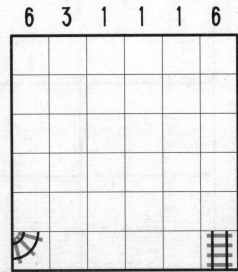

Place a number from 1 to 6 into each square, so that no number repeats in any row, column, bold-lined 3x2 box or dashed-line cage.

The numbers in each dashed-line cage must add up to the total given at the top-left of that cage.

See Number Game 42 for a solved example using numbers 1 to 4.

a)

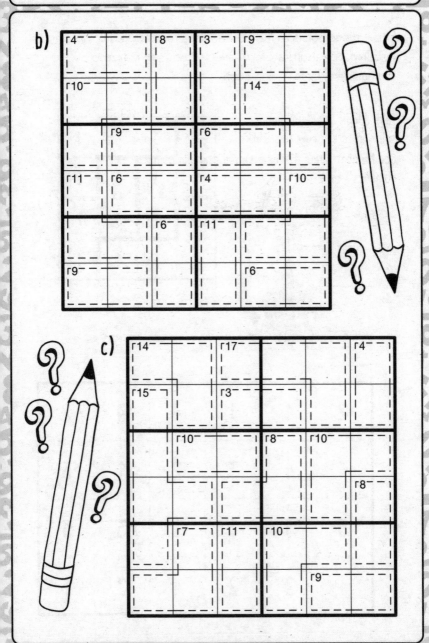

Draw along some of the dashed lines to divide each grid into six separate areas. Every area must contain the numbers 1 to 4 once each.

Take a look at this example solution to see how this works:

4	3	4	1
2	3	3	2
4	1	4	2
2	3	1	1

a)

2	4	1	4	4	2
4	4	3	2	1	3
3	3	1	1	3	3
1	2	2	4	2	1

b)

3	1	1	2	3	2
1	3	4	2	4	3
4	2	1	1	3	4
4	3	2	2	4	1

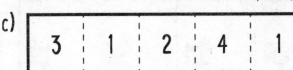

c)

3	1	2	4	1	2
1	2	2	4	3	4
2	4	3	3	1	2
3	1	4	4	1	3

Complete the grid so that each number from 1 to 16 appears once, and so that you can trace a path from 1 through to 16 simply by following the arrows from number to number. Each arrow must point in the direction of the next highest number in the path.

Take a look at the example solution to see how this works.

1 ↘	12 →	7 ↙	13 ↙
11 ↗	2 ↓	14 ↘	6 ↖
8 ↘	3 ↘	5 ↗	15 ↓
10 ↑	9 ←	4 ↑	16

1 →	↓	↙	↓
↗	↘	↘	9 ↙
3 ↘	↖	↓	↑
↗	←	11 ↖	16

All
of the
ANSWERS

NUMBER GAME 1

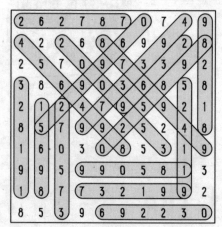

```
2 6 2 7 8 7 0 7 4 9
4 2 2 6 8 6 9 9 2 8
2 5 7 0 9 7 3 3 9 2
3 8 6 9 0 3 6 8 5 8
2 1 2 4 7 9 5 2 1 8
8 5 7 9 9 2 5 2 4 8
1 6 0 3 0 8 5 3 1 9
9 9 5 9 9 0 5 8 1 3
1 8 7 7 3 2 1 9 9 2
8 5 3 9 6 9 2 2 3 0
```

NUMBER GAME 2

16

NUMBER GAME 3

a)
```
    32
  15  17
 7   8   9
3   4   4   5
```

b)
```
    49
  25  24
 12  13  11
5   7   6   5
```

c)
```
    40
  19  21
 9   10  11
3   6   4   7
```

NUMBER GAME 4

a)
6	5	2	3	1	4
4	1	3	6	2	5
2	6	5	1	4	3
3	4	1	2	5	6
1	3	4	5	6	2
5	2	6	4	3	1

b)
1	3	6	4	5	2
5	4	2	3	1	6
2	5	4	6	3	1
3	6	1	5	2	4
6	2	3	1	4	5
4	1	5	2	6	3

c)
6	5	2	4	3	1
4	1	3	5	2	6
1	3	5	2	6	4
2	6	4	1	5	3
5	4	6	3	1	2
3	2	1	6	4	5

NUMBER GAME 5

a)

16
4
2
9
45
30

b)

5
20
4
2
6
12

NUMBER GAME 6

12 = 4 + 8

20 = 5 + 6 + 9

26 = 4 + 5 + 8 + 9

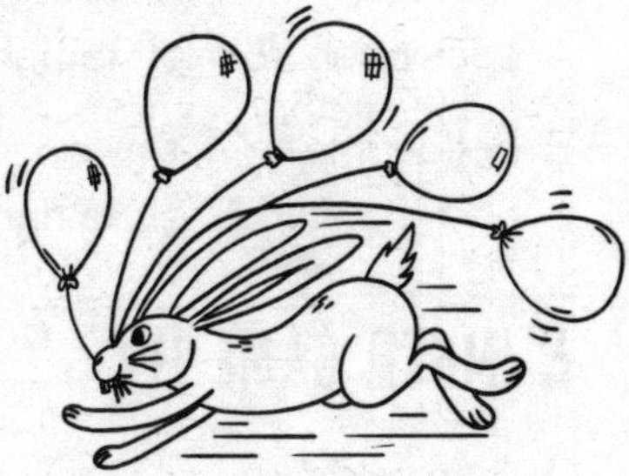

NUMBER GAME 7

You end up at the square with a letter 'I' in it:

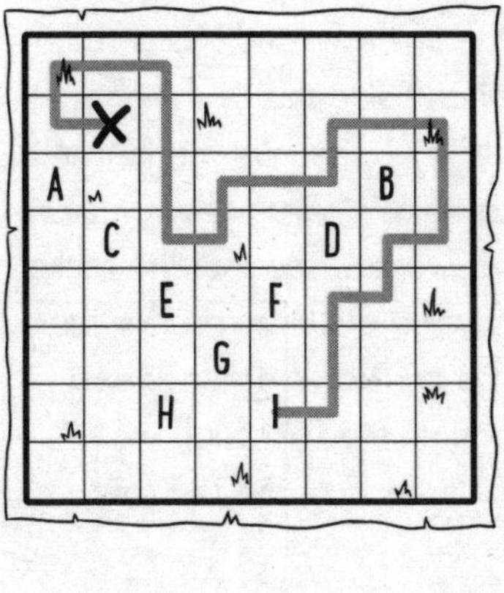

NUMBER GAME 8

14 circles: 12 around the outside, 1 in the centre and another 1 that runs through the middle of the 12 outer circles.

NUMBER GAME 9

a) 24 days

b) 31 days – since today is the 3rd of January

c) 2 days – since today must be the 27th of December

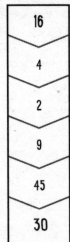

NUMBER GAME 10

a) Top shelf: 22 is missing. The number increases by 4 at each book from left to right.

b) Middle shelf: 26 is missing. The number increases by 11 at each book from left to right.

c) Bottom shelf: 44 is missing. The number decreases by 3 at each book from left to right.

NUMBER GAME 11

a) 1: it could also be a 5

b) 4, 5 or 6

c) 5: this is the highest dice face with a dot in the middle

NUMBER GAME 12

 = 7

 = 5

We can work this out by noticing that the second row has one more roller-skate than the first row, and has a value on the right-hand side that is 7 higher (since 19 - 12 = 7). This must mean that the roller-skate has a value of 7. Once we know this, we can see that the rocket must have a value of 5 in order for the first row to be correct. We don't need to use the bottom row, although we could use this instead of the first row if we wanted.

NUMBER GAME 13

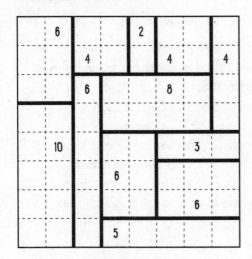

NUMBER GAME 14

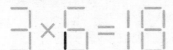 

$3 \times 6 = 18$ $2 \times 8 = 16$

NUMBER GAME 15

a)

	6	4	4	6	
7	4	3	1	2	3
3	2	1	3	4	7
5	1	4	2	3	5
5	3	2	4	1	5
	4	6	6	4	

b)

	7	3	3	7	
4	3	1	2	4	6
6	4	2	1	3	4
4	1	3	4	2	6
6	2	4	3	1	4
	3	7	7	3	

NUMBER GAME 16

Adrian is 6, Beau is 3 and Chandrika is 9.

One way to work this out is by seeing what it means for Chandrika to be 3 times as old as Beau. For this to be true there are only three options: Beau is 1 and Chandrika is 3; or Beau is 2 and Chandrika is 6; or Beau is 3 and Chandrika is 9. There are no other options because we know each age is a single digit. However, we also know that Chandrika is 6 years older than Beau, so it must be the case that Beau is 3 and Chandrika is 9. We can then use the clue about candles to work out that Adrian must be 6.

NUMBER GAME 17

a)

1	5	3 < 4	2

5 3 < 4 2 1

4 1 < 2 < 3 5

2 4 < 5 1 3

3 2 1 5 > 4

b)

5 1 3 > 2 4

2 4 1 < 3 5

4 5 2 1 3

1 3 < 4 5 2

3 2 5 4 1

c)

1 5 2 4 > 3

4 1 5 3 > 2

3 4 1 2 5

5 > 2 3 1 4

2 < 3 < 4 5 > 1

NUMBER GAME 18

a)

16	13	12	1
15	14	11	2
8	9	10	3
7	6	5	4

b)

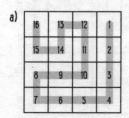

16	1	2	3
15	10	9	4
14	11	8	5
13	12	7	6

c)

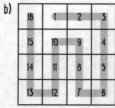

1	8	9	16
2	7	10	15
3	6	11	14
4	5	12	13

NUMBER GAME 19

a) You have an equal chance. There are four possible outcomes: heads+heads, heads+tails, tails+heads and tails+tails. Two of these have the same result, heads+heads and tails+tails. This means that out of the possible outcomes, two of them give you the same result on each toss and two of them don't give you the same result. This means they have an equal chance of occurring.

b) Option 3. You are equally likely to get either heads or tails. This is because each coin toss is completely separate from the coin toss before it, so each toss on its own has an equal chance of either heads or tails. It doesn't matter what has happened before - the coin doesn't have a 'memory'. Even though you had five heads in a row before, this doesn't affect any future toss.

NUMBER GAME 20

1	9	1	8	4
5		3		8	3	6
4	0	9	4	6		2
0		3		4		1
9		5	2	4	0	0
8	7	0		5		4
		1	8	5	6	4

NUMBER GAME 21

a) 6 circles

b) 6 stars

NUMBER GAME 22

14 = 1 + 10 + 3
19 = 2 + 6 + 11
26 = 7 + 10 + 9

NUMBER GAME 23

a)

2	2	2	🏁
🏁	🏁		2
3	3	2	🏁
🏁			🏁

b)

2	2		🏁
🏁	🏁		2
3	4	🏁	2
🏁		2	🏁

c)

2	2		🏁
🏁	🏁	2	
🏁		4	2
1		🏁	1

NUMBER GAME 24

a)

	2	3	1	4	2
3		3			1
1	1	4	3	3	3
1	4	4	4		1
2		2	2	4	2

b)

1	2	1	4	3		
1	1	4	4		3	
2	3	4	2	3	3	
3				2	2	
2	4			1	4	1

NUMBER GAME 25

28 is the odd number out, because all of the other numbers are in the 3-times table, meaning that they are whole-number multiples of 3.

NUMBER GAME 26

a) 1pm

b) 10:30am

c) 35 minutes – made up of 10 minutes for breakfast, 20 minutes for lunch, and 5 minutes for the mid-morning snack

NUMBER GAME 27

	1	3	1	2	
1	1	3		2	2
3	3	2	1		1
2	2		3	1	1
1		1	2	3	3
	2	1	2	3	

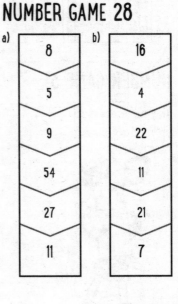

NUMBER GAME 28

a)

8
5
9
54
27
11

b)

16
4
22
11
21
7

NUMBER GAME 29

a)

0	0	1	0	1	1
0	0	1	1	0	1
1	1	0	0	1	0
0	0	1	0	1	1
1	1	0	1	0	0
1	1	0	1	0	0

b)

1	0	0	1	0	1
1	0	1	0	1	0
0	1	0	0	1	1
0	0	1	1	0	1
1	1	0	1	0	0
0	1	1	0	1	0

c)

0	0	1	0	1	1
0	0	1	0	1	1
1	1	0	1	0	0
0	1	0	1	1	0
1	0	1	0	0	1
1	1	0	1	0	0

NUMBER GAME 30

a)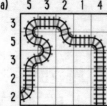

b)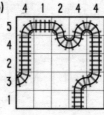

c)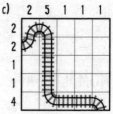

NUMBER GAME 31

The numbers add up to a total of 5:

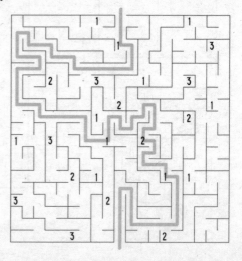

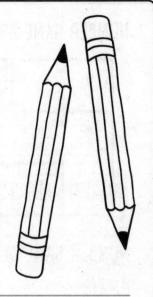

NUMBER GAME 32

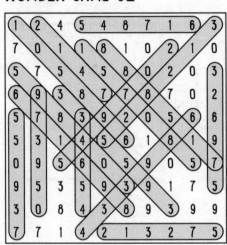

1	2	4	5	4	8	7	1	6	3
7	0	1	1	8	1	0	2	1	0
5	7	5	4	5	8	0	2	0	3
6	9	3	8	7	7	8	7	0	2
5	7	8	3	9	2	0	5	6	6
5	3	1	4	5	6	1	8	1	9
0	9	9	5	6	0	5	9	0	7
9	5	3	5	9	3	9	1	7	5
3	0	8	4	3	8	9	3	9	9
7	7	1	4	2	1	3	2	7	5

NUMBER GAME 33

a)

5	1	4	6	2	3
3	2	6	5	4	1
1	3	5	4	6	2
4	6	2	3	1	5
6	5	1	2	3	4
2	4	3	1	5	6

b)

5	2	1	4	3	6
6	4	3	5	2	1
1	3	5	6	4	2
4	6	2	3	1	5
2	5	4	1	6	3
3	1	6	2	5	4

c)

4	2	1	5	3	6
3	5	6	4	2	1
1	3	5	6	4	2
6	4	2	3	1	5
5	1	3	2	6	4
2	6	4	1	5	3

NUMBER GAME 34

a)

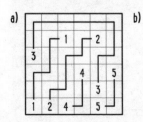

b)

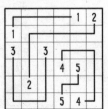

c)

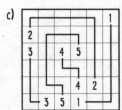

NUMBER GAME 35

a)

3÷ 3	1	9+ 2
2	3	1
1	6× 2	3

b)

18× 3	1	6× 2
2× 1	2	3
2	3	1

NUMBER GAME 36

a) 22 blocks

b) 18 blocks

c) 12 blocks

NUMBER GAME 37

1 ⬇	5 ➡	6 ➡	7 ⬇
2 ⬊	15 ⬊	9 ⬋	8 ⬅
13 ➡	11 ⬇	14 ⬉	4 ⬉
10 ⬈	12 ⬋	3 ⬈	16

NUMBER GAME 38

16 sides

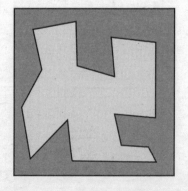

NUMBER GAME 39

a)

2	4	1	2
3	3	1	3
1	1	4	3
4	4	2	2

b)

1	4	1	2
2	3	2	3
1	1	3	4
4	3	4	2

c)

1	2	4	4
3	4	3	1
4	2	3	3
2	1	1	2

NUMBER GAME 40

a)
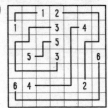

b)
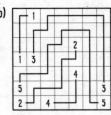

c)
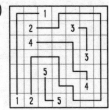

NUMBER GAME 41

a)

57

26	31

14	12	19

9	5	7	12

6	3	2	5	7

b)

78

42	36

23	19	17

12	11	8	9

7	5	6	2	7

c)

65

34	31

19	15	16

10	9	6	10

4	6	3	3	7

NUMBER GAME 42

a)
2	4	3	1
3	1	2	4
4	3	1	2
1	2	4	3

b)
2	3	1	4
1	4	2	3
4	2	3	1
3	1	4	2

c)
4	2	3	1
3	1	4	2
2	4	1	3
1	3	2	4

NUMBER GAME 43

	3	1	2	3	
3	3	1	2		2
1	1	2		3	3
2	2		3	1	1
3		3	1	2	2
	2	3	1	2	

NUMBER GAME 44

NUMBER GAME 45

a)
9	3	6	1	8	5	2	4	7
7	5	8	2	4	9	3	6	1
2	1	4	3	6	7	9	5	8
6	4	1	5	7	2	8	9	3
8	7	3	6	9	1	5	2	4
5	9	2	4	3	8	1	7	6
1	6	5	8	2	4	7	3	9
3	8	9	7	5	6	4	1	2
4	2	7	9	1	3	6	8	5

b)
1	2	8	3	9	5	4	7	6
6	9	4	8	2	7	5	3	1
3	5	7	4	6	1	2	8	9
8	1	5	2	7	6	3	9	4
9	7	3	5	1	4	6	2	8
4	6	2	9	3	8	1	5	7
7	4	9	6	5	2	8	1	3
2	3	6	1	8	9	7	4	5
5	8	1	7	4	3	9	6	2

NUMBER GAME 46

11 stars: 7 in a chain from top-left to bottom-right, plus 2 more to the top-right and 2 more to the bottom-left.

NUMBER GAME 47

You end up at the square with a letter 'A' in it:

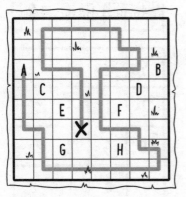

NUMBER GAME 49

25 = 8 + 17
36 = 4 + 14 + 18
47 = 4 + 8 + 17 + 18

NUMBER GAME 48

a)

25	22	21	20	19
24	23	8	9	18
1	6	7	10	17
2	5	12	11	16
3	4	13	14	15

b)

5	6	7	24	23
4	1	8	25	22
3	2	9	20	21
12	11	10	19	18
13	14	15	16	17

c)

5	4	3	2	1
6	7	8	9	10
19	18	17	16	11
20	21	22	15	12
25	24	23	14	13

NUMBER GAME 50

36 is the odd number out, because all of the other numbers are made up of digits that add up to 10. For example, 19 is made up of 1 and 9, and 1+9=10; or 802 is made up of 8, 0 and 2, and 8+0+2=10, too.

NUMBER GAME 51

a)

6× 2	3	5+ 1	4
4× 1	6+ 2	4	6× 3
4	4+ 1	3	2
12× 3	4	2÷ 2	1

b)

72× 2	4	3	4× 1
3	1− 1	8× 2	4
3− 1	2	4	18× 3
4	3	1	2

c)

6× 1	3	2÷ 4	2
6× 3	2	1	4× 4
2	12+ 4	3	1
5+ 4	1	2	3

d)

24× 3	2	4	4÷ 1
8× 2	1	18× 3	4
4÷ 1	4	2	3
4	6× 3	1	2

NUMBER GAME 52

12 = 5 + 1 + 6
25 = 8 + 11 + 6
30 = 7 + 11 + 12

NUMBER GAME 53

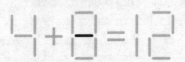 4 + 8 = 12   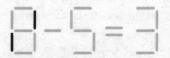 8 − 5 = 3

NUMBER GAME 54

	8		4	6	6	4
8	1	5	0		6	
	6		2		8	
	6	8	8	0	7	
	4		6		2	
	6		9	9	0	2
9	3	8	6		9	

NUMBER GAME 55

a) 10am

b) 3pm – the time in Los Angeles is 3 hours behind that in New York City

c) 2pm – Egypt is 2 hours ahead of Britain, which is 3 hours ahead of Brazil, for a total time difference of 5 hours ahead

NUMBER GAME 56

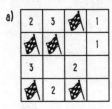

a)

2	3	🏁	1
🏁	🏁		1
3		2	
🏁	2	🏁	

b)

	🏁	2	🏁
1			2
	1		🏁
1	🏁	2	1

c)

2	🏁		🏁	1
3	🏁	4		3
🏁		2	🏁	🏁
🏁	4			🏁
🏁	3	🏁	2	1

NUMBER GAME 57

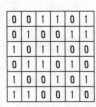

a)

0	0	1	0	1	1
1	1	0	0	1	0
0	1	0	1	0	1
0	0	1	1	0	1
1	1	0	0	1	0
1	0	1	1	0	0

b)

0	0	1	1	0	1
0	1	0	0	1	1
1	0	1	1	0	0
0	1	1	0	1	0
1	0	0	1	0	1
1	1	0	0	1	0

c)

1	0	0	1	0	0	1	1
0	0	1	0	1	1	0	1
0	1	1	0	0	1	1	0
1	0	0	1	1	0	0	1
0	1	1	0	1	0	1	0
0	0	1	1	0	1	0	1
1	1	0	1	0	0	1	0
1	1	0	0	1	1	0	0

NUMBER GAME 58

a)

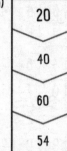

			4	11			
	13 22	4	9	5			
5	5	7	3 2	1	12		
12	8	4	9 23	4	5	11	
19	9	2	8	10 17	7	3	
	18	1	9	8	2	1 1	
		24	6	9	2	7	

b)

		13	9	11	4	6	
	20 1	1	9	5	3	2	
10	1	9	10 7	2	1	4	
	6	3	2	1	12		
3	6 6	1	3	2			
7	1	2	4	10 5	9	1	
15	2	4	3	5	1		

NUMBER GAME 59

a)

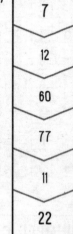

| 20 |
| 40 |
| 60 |
| 54 |
| 9 |
| 3 |

b)

| 7 |
| 12 |
| 60 |
| 77 |
| 11 |
| 22 |

NUMBER GAME 60

 = 3

 = 4

 = 8

We can work this out by noticing that the top and bottom rows are very similar, except that in the bottom row we have added a rocket to the left-hand side and ended up with a total that is 4 higher on the right-hand side. This must mean that the rocket has a value of 4. Once we know this, we can use the second row to work out that the roller-skate has a value of 3, since it must have a value that results in 7 once it is added to the 4 for the rocket. And finally we can use any of the other rows in a similar way to work out that the wheel has a value of 8.

NUMBER GAME 61

a)

	1		1		2
4	4		1	4	2
2	2		4	2	3
	3	1	4	1	3
1	4	3	3	3	2

b)

1	1	1	5	6	2	6	1
5	5	4	2		2	4	1
3	5	3	5	5	4	3	2
3	6	1	5	4	4	6	4
1	3	3	1	2			2
	3	5	6	6	4	6	2
	3	2	4			6	

NUMBER GAME 62

a)

4	3	1	2	5
5 > 4	2 < 3	1
3	1	4 < 5	2
2	5	3	1	4
1 < 2	5	4 > 3

b)

2	5 > 3	4	1
5	1 < 2	3	4
4	3	1	5	2
1	4	5	2 < 3
3 > 2	4 > 1	5

c)

4	3	2	1	5
3	4	1	5	2
5	1 < 3	2	4
1	2 < 5	4	3
2	5 > 4	3	1

NUMBER GAME 63

a)

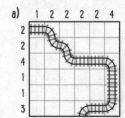

b)

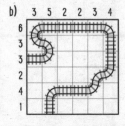

c)

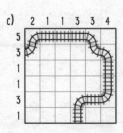

NUMBER GAME 64

a)

6	2	1	4	5	3
5	3	4	6	2	1
3	1	6	2	4	5
2	4	5	3	1	6
4	5	3	1	6	2
1	6	2	5	3	4

b)

5	4	6	1	3	2
3	1	2	4	5	6
1	2	5	3	6	4
6	3	4	2	1	5
4	5	3	6	2	1
2	6	1	5	4	3

c)

1	2	5	3	6	4
3	4	6	2	5	1
2	6	1	5	4	3
5	3	4	6	1	2
6	1	3	4	2	5
4	5	2	1	3	6

NUMBER GAME 65

a)

				6	4
				7	3

b)

5				4	
5					
				6	

NUMBER GAME 66

4 times: the two creases shown in the example,
then it was folded in half again two more times.

NUMBER GAME 67

a)
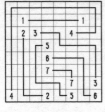

b)
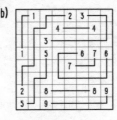

c)
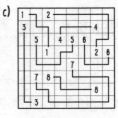

NUMBER GAME 68

a)

b)

c)

NUMBER GAME 69

2	7	2	5	2	6	6	2	3	2	7	3
4	6	4	9	9	3	7	9	9	7	0	0
1	3	1	2	2	7	9	4	5	2	2	3
2	1	9	9	0	3	5	6	1	2	8	0
8	2	1	7	7	9	5	1	0	5	1	9
7	1	0	9	5	6	5	4	5	8	9	5
5	4	1	0	6	5	4	8	5	2	3	5
7	5	0	5	3	2	1	4	4	9	4	0
0	1	0	4	9	6	9	4	9	9	7	2
4	4	1	1	1	1	2	8	7	1	1	1
3	9	1	2	4	6	8	6	6	2	5	2
0	0	2	3	2	2	5	0	1	4	2	8

NUMBER GAME 70

a)

- 12: they could both be 6s
- 6: there might be no dots missing, making them a 2 and a 4

b)

- 12: they could both be 6s
- 8: the first must be a 6, but the second could be a 2

NUMBER GAME 71

a)

	1			4	2
1	4		2	2	
3	4	3	4		2
3	1	3	1	3	2
4	2	3	1	1	4

b)

4	3	2	5	1	3	1	
1	6	5	6	5	4	1	6
		5	2	5	3	1	6
6	5		6	6	1	4	3
	2	3	3	4		3	4
6		1	3	1	2	2	4
4	2	4		5	5	2	2

NUMBER GAME 72

a)

6	3	2	9	5	8	4	1	7
4	5	7	1	3	6	8	9	2
8	1	9	7	4	2	6	5	3
3	6	8	2	1	7	5	4	9
2	9	1	4	6	5	3	7	8
7	4	5	8	9	3	2	6	1
5	2	3	6	7	9	1	8	4
9	8	4	5	2	1	7	3	6
1	7	6	3	8	4	9	2	5

b)

2	4	6	3	1	7	8	5	9
7	8	9	5	2	4	3	1	6
3	5	1	9	8	6	2	4	7
5	6	8	1	7	9	4	2	3
4	3	2	8	6	5	7	9	1
9	1	7	4	3	2	5	6	8
8	7	5	2	9	1	6	3	4
6	9	4	7	5	3	1	8	2
1	2	3	6	4	8	9	7	5

NUMBER GAME 73

a) 63 days: this is made up of 26 days in May, 30 in June and 7 in July.

b) 372 days: this is made up of 365 days in a year, 5 days until the 3rd April and then 2 days until 5th April.

c) 107 days: today is the 16th September, so this is made up of 15 previous days in September, 31 days in August, 31 days in July, and 30 days in June.

NUMBER GAME 74

a) Top shelf: 8 is missing. The number doubles in value at each book from left to right.

b) Middle shelf: 1 is missing. The number divides in value by 3 at each book from left to right.

c) Bottom shelf: 107 is missing. The number decreases by 14 at each book from left to right.

NUMBER GAME 75

a)

			24	16	9	16
		25/24	8	7	9	1
	24/20	8	7	9	9/6	9
24	8	7	9	6/	2	4
14	5	9	16/6	1	3	2
6	6	12/5	9	2	1	
16	1	5	7	3		

b)

	19	4	8	10		
24	9	3	8	4	3/	
4/	3	1	11/	2	1	22
5/	5	17/11	5	3	2	1
15	2	9	3	1	8/6	8
	9/	8	1	14/9	5	9
		16	2	9	1	4

NUMBER GAME 76

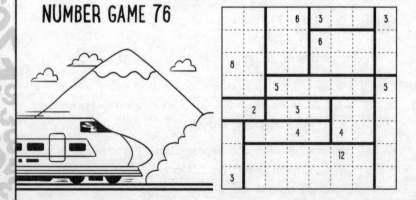

NUMBER GAME 77

a)

	3	11	7	7	7	7	
10	1	5	4	2	3	6	11
11	2	6	3	5	4	1	10
7	4	1	2	3	6	5	14
14	6	3	5	4	1	2	7
11	3	2	6	1	5	4	10
10	5	4	1	6	2	3	11
	8	6	7	7	7	7	

b)

	9	9	3	7	9	5	
13	6	5	2	1	4	3	8
8	3	4	1	6	5	2	13
7	1	2	4	3	6	5	14
14	5	6	3	2	1	4	7
8	2	1	5	4	3	6	13
13	4	3	6	5	2	1	8
	6	4	11	9	5	7	

NUMBER GAME 78

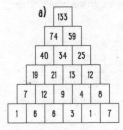

a)

```
            133
          74    59
        40   34   25
      19   21   13   12
    7    12   9    4    8
  1    6    6    3    1    7
```

b)

```
            173
          78    95
        32   46   49
      12   20   26   23
    4    8    12   14   9
  1    3    5    7    7    2
```

c)

```
            80
          45    35
        24   21   14
      11   13   8    6
    4    7    6    2    4
  2    2    5    1    1    3
```

NUMBER GAME 79

a)

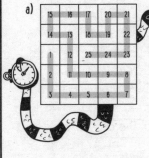

15	16	17	20	21
14	13	18	19	22
1	12	25	24	23
2	11	10	9	8
3	4	5	6	7

b)

9	8	7	6	5
10	1	2	3	4
11	16	17	24	23
12	15	18	25	22
13	14	19	20	21

c)

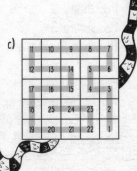

11	10	9	8	7
12	13	14	5	6
17	16	15	4	3
18	25	24	23	2
19	20	21	22	1

NUMBER GAME 80

a)
```
3  4  1  2  6 > 5
1  5  4 > 3  2  6
4  1  5  6  3  2
6  2  3  4  5  1
2 < 3  6 > 5  1  4
5  6 > 2 > 1  4  3
```

b)
```
6  3  4  1 < 2  5
3  6  2  5  1  4
4 < 5  6  2  3  1
1 < 4  5  3  6  2
2  1  3  4 < 5  6
5  2  1  6  4  3
```

c)
```
5  1  4 > 2  6 > 3
1  3  6 > 4  5  2
3 < 6  2 > 1  4  5
6  4  3  5 > 2  1
4 > 2  5  3  1  6
2  5  1  6  3 < 4
```

NUMBER GAME 81

Diego is 10, Eva is 6 and Freya is 12. One way to work this out is by seeing what it means for Eva to be half as old as Freya. For this to be true there are only four options given the age range of 5 to 16: Eva is 5 and Freya is 10; Eva is 6 and Freya is 12; Eva is 7 and Freya is 14; or Eva is 8 and Freya is 16. We also know that the ages of all three children add up to 28, so we can write this information in a table which also includes the age of Diego that would be required in order for the ages to add to 28:

	Diego's age	Eva's age	Freya's age
Possibility 1	13	5	10
Possibility 2	10	6	12
Possibility 3	7	7	14
Possibility 4	4	8	16

We can immediately eliminate possibility 4 because Diego would be too young. If we also remember that Diego is two years younger than Freya, we can see that the answer must be possibility 2.

NUMBER GAME 82

The numbers add up to a total of 40:

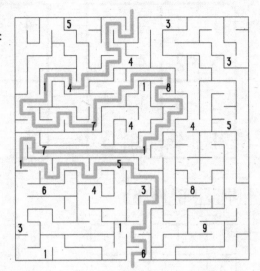

NUMBER GAME 83

a) 1 in 6. This is easy to work out if you think of it this way: Imagine that the first dice roll is picking you a random number, from 1 to 6. The second dice roll now has a 1 in 6 chance of matching that random number you just picked. So the overall chance of rolling the same number on both dice must be 1 in 6 too.

b) The maximum possible total is 18, and the lowest possible total is 3. That's because the highest number you can roll on each dice is 6, so if you rolled three 6s that would be 6+6+6=18. The lowest number you can roll on each dice is 1, so if you rolled three 1s that would be 1+1+1=3.

NUMBER GAME 84

a)

1	4	3	2
③	2	4	1
2	3	1	④
4	1	2	3

b)

4	2	1	3
1	③	4	2
2	4	③	1
3	1	2	4

NUMBER GAME 85

a)

20× 5	4	9+ 3	4× 1	2
12× 4	1	5	2	60× 3
1	30× 5	2	3	4
3	7+ 2	16× 1	4	5
2	3	4	5× 5	1

b)

11+ 2	4÷ 1	4	12+ 3	5
1	3	5	4	2- 2
2- 3	2- 2	1	5	4
5	80× 4	18× 3	2	1
4	5	2÷ 2	1	3

c)

4- 1	5+ 2	4÷ 4	2- 3	5
5	3	1	16+ 4	8× 2
6× 3	5	2	1	4
2	4	15× 3	10× 5	3× 1
4× 4	1	5	2	3

d)

11+ 5	1	24× 3	4	6× 2
6× 1	5	40× 4	2	3
3	2	5	4× 1	4
6+ 4	12× 3	2	13+ 5	1
2	4	1	3	5

NUMBER GAME 86

20 = 7 + 10 + 3
33 = 12 + 13 + 8
38 = 14 + 9 + 15

NUMBER GAME 87

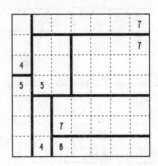

NUMBER GAME 88

	3	3	2	3	1	
3	3		2		1	1
2	2	3	1			1
1	1	2		3		3
1		1		2	3	3
3			3	1	2	2
	1	1	3	1	2	

NUMBER GAME 89

17 = 8 + 9
25 = 3 + 4 + 7 + 11
32 = 4 + 8 + 9 + 11

NUMBER GAME 90

a) 4×4 grid:

2	🏴	🏴	1
2	🏴	3	
2			1
🏴	2	🏴	1

b) 5×5 grid:

🏴	🏴		2	2
3	3	3	🏴	🏴
		🏴	5	4
2		🏴	🏴	🏴
🏴	2	2	4	🏴

c) 5×5 grid:

🏴	2	2		1
1		🏴	🏴	1
	3		3	
🏴	🏴		🏴	2
2	2		2	🏴

NUMBER GAME 91

a) 38 blocks   b) 32 blocks   c) 22 blocks

NUMBER GAME 92

```
6 9 7       1 4 4 8
2   1       9       5
9 4 1       0     7 9 5
    8 8   4 4 4     8
2 0 9             9 4 2
0   8 2   5 2 9
2 1 2     8     5 0 4
    6       3     9   7
    7 5 6 9       3 7 2
```

NUMBER GAME 93

4 times: one way is to fold it in half diagonally at each step, creating the pattern shown

---

NUMBER GAME 94

a)

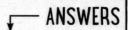

12	7				17	7
8	**4**	12		14	**9**	**5**
4	**1**	**9**	19 8	**9**	**8**	**2**
	2	**3**	**1**	**5**		
		10	**5**	3	8	
3 17		**4**	**2**	**1**	**3**	3
1	**8**	**6**	7	**2**	**4**	**1**
2	**9**			3	**1**	**2**

b)

		6			10	7
2	**2**	28	6	6	**2**	**4**
17	**4**	**8**	**5**	4 15	**1**	**3**
	11 30	**5**	**1**	**2**	**3**	
17	**8**	**9**	8 5	**1**	**4**	
17 4	**7**	**6**	**1**	**3**	7	
7	**1**	**6**	21	**7**	**9**	**5**
12	**3**	**9**			2	**2**

NUMBER GAME 95

1	0	0	1	0	1
0	1	1	0	1	0
0	0	1	0	1	1
1	0	0	1	0	1
0	1	1	0	1	0
1	1	0	1	0	0

1	1	0	0	1	0	0	1
0	1	0	0	1	0	1	1
0	0	1	1	0	1	1	0
1	1	0	1	0	1	0	0
1	0	1	0	1	0	0	1
0	0	1	1	0	1	1	0
0	1	0	0	1	0	1	1
1	0	1	1	0	1	0	0

1	0	0	1	0	0	1	1
0	0	1	0	1	1	0	1
0	1	0	1	0	1	1	0
1	0	1	0	1	0	0	1
0	1	0	1	0	1	1	0
1	0	1	0	1	0	0	1
0	1	1	0	1	0	1	0
1	1	0	1	0	1	0	0

NUMBER GAME 96

1 + 6 = 7   6 × 8 = 48

NUMBER GAME 97

4	2	3	1	5	6
1	5	6	4	2	3
2	6	1	5	3	4
5	3	4	2	6	1
3	1	5	6	4	2
6	4	2	3	1	5

NUMBER GAME 98

a)
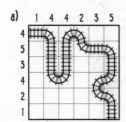

b)
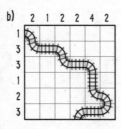

c)
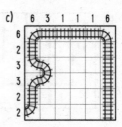

NUMBER GAME 99

a)

r5			r11		r4		r12	
2	6	5	3	1	4
3	r7 4	1	2	r10 6	5
r7 6	1	r5 2	r6 5	4	3
r10 4	r7 5	3	1	r8 2	6
5	2	r13 4	6	3	r3 1
1	r9 3	6	4	5	2

b)

r4		r8		r3		r9		
3	1	6	2	5	4
4	r10 5	2	1	r14 6	3
1	r9 6	3	r6 4	2	5
r11 5	r6 2	4	r4 3	1	r10 6
2	r6 4	5	r11 8	3	1
r9 6	3	1	5	r6 4	2

c)

r14		r17				r4	
6	3	2	5	4	1
r15 4	5	1	2	6	3
2	r10 6	4	1	3	5
5	1	r3 3	4	2	r8 6
3	r7 4	r11 5	r10 6	1	2
1	2	6	3	r9 5	4

NUMBER GAME 100

a)

2	4	1	4	4	2
4	4	3	2	1	3
3	3	3	1	3	3
1	2	2	4	2	1

b)

3	1	1	2	3	2
1	3	4	2	4	3
4	2	1	1	3	4
4	3	2	2	4	1

c)

3	1	2	4	1	2
1	2	2	4	3	4
2	4	3	3	1	2
3	1	4	4	1	3

NUMBER GAME 101

1 ⮕	14 ⬇	2 ⬋	8 ⬇
13 ⬈	15 ⬊	6 ⬊	9 ⬋
3 ⬊	12 ⬉	10 ⬇	7 ⬆
5 ⬈	4 ⬅	11 ⬋	16

NOTES
AND
SCRIBBLES

ALSO AVAILABLE:

ISBN 9781780559155

ISBN 9781780558738

ISBN 9781780558264

ISBN 9781780558721

ISBN 9781780557403

ISBN 9781780557106

ISBN 9781780556642

ISBN 9781780556635

ISBN 9781780556628

ISBN 9781780556543

ISBN 9781780556659

ISBN 9781780556192

ISBN 9781780556208

ISBN 9781780555935

ISBN 9781780555638

ISBN 9781780554730

ISBN 9781780555621

ISBN 9781780554723

ISBN 9781780555409

ISBN 9781780553146

ISBN 9781780553085

ISBN 9781780553078

ISBN 9781780552491